Enjoy these other family devotionals published by Zondervan:

Hurlbut's Story of the Bible
Meet the Calderwoods
Through-the-Bible Storybook
The Zondervan Bible Storybook

Kwitcher-BellYakin

Devotions for Young Families

BONNIE BRUNO

ZondervanPublishingHouse

Grand Rapids, Michigan

A Division of HarperCollinsPublishers

Kwitcherbellyakin
Copyright © 1992 by Bonnie Bruno

Requests for information should be addressed to:
Zondervan Publishing House
Grand Rapids, Michigan 49530

Library of Congress Cataloging-in-Publication Data

Bruno, Bonnie
    Kwitcherbellyakin : devotions for young families / Bonnie Bruno.
        p. cm.
    Summary: Accounts of everyday situations are accompanied by
questions and prayer activities that encourage reflection on God's
presence in our lives.
    ISBN 0-310-54811-X (alk. paper)
    1. Family—Prayer-books and devotions—English. 2. Children—
Prayer-books and devotions—English. 3. Christian life—Juvenile
literature. [1. Prayer books and devotions. 2. Christian life. 3.
Conduct of life.] I. Title.
BV255.B75 1992
249—dc20   91–39388
                                                               CIP
                                                               AC

All Scripture quotations, unless otherwise noted, are taken from the
HOLY BIBLE: NEW INTERNATIONAL VERSION® (North American
Edition). Copyright © 1973, 1978, 1984, by the International Bible
Society. Used by permission of Zondervan Publishing House.

"NIV" and "New International Version" are registered in the United
States Patent and Trademark Office by the International Bible
Society.

Edited by Joyce K. Ellis
Cover design by Lecy Design
Interior design by Rachel Hostetter
Interior illustrations by Win Mumma

Printed in the United States of America

92 93 94 95 96 97 / AM / 10 9 8 7 6 5 4 3 2 1

Dedicated to the ones
who've encouraged me most—
Nick, Nick Jr., and Carrie

CONTENTS

▶▶▶▶▶▶▶▶▶▶▶▶▶▶▶▶▶▶▶▶▶▶▶▶▶▶

INTRODUCTION
▶▶▶▶▶▶▶▶▶▶▶▶▶▶▶▶▶▶▶▶▶▶▶▶▶▶▶▶▶

The seed for *Kwitcherbellyakin* was planted during a memorable family camping trip several years ago. We'd barely unpacked the two million items needed for such an excursion when the rains began.

Within ten minutes, we were forced inside our spacious orange tent, which did not live up to its waterproof reputation. High winds whipped the nylon as puddles began forming inside at each corner. Within a short time, the wind increased dramatically and lightning crackled overhead.

What to do? Run for better cover, of course. One by one, we raced through the darkness to the nearest vehicle, praying that our favorite camping spot (on a wooded hill overlooking the lake) wouldn't attract the next lightning bolt. My husband and I ended up shivering in the pickup. Our son and daughter, a bit more organized in their escape, grabbed blankets, pillows, and cassette tapes to get them through the ordeal. But we were not happy campers.

When the unexpected disrupts our plans, we've noticed it's always easier to complain than to praise God. It's always easier to see the bad in a situation than the good we can learn from it. As you read these devotional thoughts together, why not date the prayers you write at the end of each one so that your family can watch God at work? Every couple of weeks take time to review and share the joy of answered prayer. Let the children take turns filling in the date and the way in which God answered each request. Why ask unless we *expect* an answer?

Someone has wisely written, "He who forgets the language of gratitude can never be on speaking terms with happiness." In other words, "Kwitcherbellyakin!" God—and your children—deserve much more.

1

KWITCHER-BELLYAKIN

Jennifer and her friends sat around in her tree house, talking about which season of the year they liked best. "My favorite is summer," Sonya told them. "That's when I spend a month with my grandparents. We usually go camping in the mountains while I'm there."

"Summer's OK," agreed Ty, "but sometimes it gets too hot. I like spring better because it's warmer than winter but cooler than summer."

His sister Jennifer shrugged. "I like all four seasons," she said. "But I really love the way the air smells at football games in the fall—kind of cold and crispy."

Ty jabbed his sister. "Cold and crispy?" he teased. "That sounds like leftover chicken."

Chad laughed. "I like the fall, too, especially when the leaves turn orange and gold."

"Ugh!" moaned Jennifer. "That's the only part I don't like about fall—having to rake leaves."

"Kwitcherbellyakin, Jennifer," Chad scolded.

"If it weren't for this old oak tree, you wouldn't have a tree house to play in all summer."

"Or shade over your picnic table," Sonya reminded her.

"That's right," said Ty. "Without that tree, we'd have a big bare spot in our backyard."

Jennifer looked out the door of the tree house at the thick trunk of the oak below them. "I guess you're right," she said. "But I sure wouldn't have any leaves to rake, either, would I?"

> **By him all things were created.**
>
> Colossians 1:16

▶▶▶▶▶▶▶▶▶▶▶▶▶

Something to Remember

God created good things, like trees, for me to enjoy.

Questions for Family Discussion

1. Which season do you like best?
2. What kind of good things has God given you?
3. Do you ever take your favorite things for granted?

Write a Family Prayer

_____

_____

_____

Kwitcherbellyakin

2

>>>>>>>>>>>>>>>>>>>>>>>>>>>>>>>>>>>>>

RIGHT ON TIME

One early Saturday morning, Grandpa tapped his grandson on the shoulder. "Get up, Tom," he whispered. "We have an important appointment to keep, remember?"

Tom turned over and pressed his face into the fluffy pillow. "It's too cold, Grandpa," he mumbled. "Besides, I haven't finished sleeping yet."

"You look awake enough to me." Grandpa chuckled. "Now hurry or we'll be late."

Grandpa and Tom pulled on their boots, zipped their jackets, and tiptoed out the kitchen door. There, on the top step of the porch, they shared a cup of hot cocoa Grandpa had waiting for them.

Tom yawned. "When will the sun come up?" he asked.

Grandpa searched the sky for clues. "In a couple of minutes," he said.

A cool breeze tickled Tom's nose. Leaning forward, he folded his arms on top of his knees and rested his head. Birds rustled in the berry

RIGHT ON TIME   **15**

bushes nearby. Toads croaked from their home by the creek.

"It won't be long now," said Grandpa.

First they saw the sky turn a pale pink, the color of Mom's terry cloth bathrobe. They watched the color swirl and deepen until it became a bright pinkish purple.

"Get ready, son!" said Grandpa, patting Tom on the back.

Tom looked up but quickly had to turn away. The sun's fiery orange face had popped over the hill, spilling brightness everywhere.

Grandpa glanced at his old silver watch. "Seven minutes past five," he said. He put his arm around Tom's shoulder. "God is right on time this morning—as usual."

> **This is the day the LORD has made; let us rejoice and be glad in it.**
>
> Psalm 118:24

▶▶▶▶▶▶▶▶▶▶▶▶

Something to Remember

God is never late.

Questions for Family Discussion

1. Have you ever crawled out of bed early enough to watch a sunrise? How did it make you feel?
2. Can you think of other ways in which God is right on time?

Kwitcherbellyakin

3. How can we show our appreciation to God for each new day?

Write a Family Prayer

_____

_____

_____

_____

3

▸▸▸▸▸▸▸▸▸▸▸▸▸▸▸▸▸▸▸▸▸▸▸▸▸▸▸▸▸▸▸▸▸▸▸▸▸▸▸

A PEANUT-
BUTTER FEAST

One day Peter found his mother fixing a tall stack of peanut-butter-and-jelly sandwiches. "Peanut butter *again?*" he grumbled. "Why can't I have something like tuna or bologna?"

"You can," replied Mother, wrapping the sandwiches in foil. "There's a can of tuna in the cabinet over there."

Peter stood there, puzzled. Why was Mom putting the sandwiches in a bag?

"We're taking these to some homeless people who live in the park," she explained. "It's a special project for my Sunday school class."

"But how do you know they'll like peanut butter?" asked Peter. "I mean, it's hardly a feast or anything."

Mom scowled. "Peanut butter might taste like a feast when you're cold and hungry, Peter."

Peter shrugged. "I guess so," he said. Peter thought of the people at the park. He remembered seeing an old man there once, huddled under a raggedy blanket. Nearby, a woman sat leaning

Kwitcherbellyakin

against a tree and talking to a dog that had stopped to lick her hand. All of her belongings were stuffed into a big black garbage bag.

Peter looked up at his mother. "Do you think I could go to the park with you?" he asked.

"Sure," Mom said. "We could use all the help we can get."

Peter helped his mother put the wrapped sandwiches into a paper sack. "Mom, why are they there?"

Mom shook her head sadly. "God only knows," she said. "But we can show a little of His love by bringing these sandwiches to them."

Peter stuck his finger in the peanut butter jar for a taste. "Mom," he said quietly. "Forget the tuna. I guess peanut butter will be fine for me, too."

> **The eyes of all look to you,**
> **and you give them their food**
> **at the proper time.**
>
> Psalm 145:15

▶▶▶▶▶▶▶▶▶▶▶▶▶

Something to Remember

God gives me my daily food.

Questions for Family Discussion

1. Do you ever get tired of certain foods?
2. Can you imagine what it feels like to be home-less?
3. How does God provide for our daily needs?

Write a Family Prayer

_____

_____

_____

_____

Kwitcherbellyakin

4

>>>>>>>>>>>>>>>>>>>>>>>>>>>>>>>>>>>>>>>

WHEN EVERYTHING GOES WRONG

One morning Meg decided to surprise her parents. *I'll make them a special breakfast and take it to their room*, she thought.

First Meg popped two pieces of bread into the toaster. A few minutes later, she smelled smoke. The toast looked as black as her cat, Ralph, who sat meowing for his own breakfast.

Meg sighed in frustration. "I'll make them cereal instead," she said, tossing the toast in the garbage. But Meg discovered that the carton of milk in the refrigerator had soured.

Next, as she was pouring two glasses of orange juice, she tripped over Ralph's dish. She lost her balance, and juice flew in all directions.

After cleaning up the sticky mess, she slumped at the counter. *There's nothing left to fix*, she thought.

Then she had an idea.

Meg hurried to the china cabinet and took out

a pair of rose-trimmed plates. Then she went to the refrigerator. Soon she was tiptoeing down the hall, balancing her surprise breakfast on a tray, complete with a vase of silk flowers.

When Meg saw the look of delight on Daddy's face, she nearly forgot about the burned toast, spilled orange juice, and sour milk.

"Pizza!" exclaimed Daddy. "And a big glass of cola."

Daddy shook Mom gently. "Wake up," he said. "It's breakfast time, and guess who surprised us?"

Mom sat up and rubbed her eyes. "Oh, thank you, Meg," she said sleepily. "This looks scrumptious."

Daddy and Mom each gave her a gigantic thank-you hug.

"What a breakfast!" they cried.

> When anxiety was great within
> me, your consolation brought
> joy to my soul.
>
> Psalm 94:19

▶▶▶▶▶▶▶▶▶▶▶▶▶

Something to Remember
God gives me special hugs.

Questions for Family Discussion
1. Can you remember a time when your plans didn't work out right?

Kwitcherbellyakin

2. Have you ever given up? Did you regret it later?
3. How can we encourage someone who's having a not-so-good day?
4. How does God give us hugs?

Write a Family Prayer

_____

_____

_____

_____

5

▶▶▶▶▶▶▶▶▶▶▶▶▶▶▶▶▶▶▶▶▶▶▶▶▶▶▶▶▶▶▶▶

TOUGH DECISION

"What should I do?" Michael asked his dad. "If I decide to spend the night with Jake, I'll miss seeing Robbie. But if I stay home to see Robbie, Jake will be mad."

Dad thought for a moment. "Well, Michael," he said, "the choice is really yours. But I seem to remember hearing you promise Jake that you would help him celebrate his birthday tomorrow. Besides, you'll get to see Robbie next weekend when we camp at the lake."

Michael cupped his chin in his hands and stared across the breakfast table. "Jake's a good friend," he admitted, "and I did promise him I'd spend the night for his birthday. But Robbie's my cousin, and that's almost like a *best* friend." Michael tossed up his hands. "I give up," he moaned. "One of them is going to be upset with me no matter what I decide. Isn't there a verse somewhere in the Bible that could tell me what to do?" he asked his dad.

"Well, not directly, but maybe this one would help." Dad thumbed through the pages of his big black Bible. Then he slid it across the table to Michael, pointing to Proverbs 17:17.

Michael read the verse to himself. "A friend loves at all times." He nodded. "I think I need to make a phone call, Dad," he said, hurrying into the living room. "I want to remind Robbie to bring his baseball and glove to the campground next weekend."

> **Teach me knowledge and good judgment, for I believe in your commands.**
>
> Psalm 119:66

▶▶▶▶▶▶▶▶▶▶▶▶▶▶▶

Something to Remember

God's Word is like a map, telling me which way to turn.

Questions for Family Discussion

1. Can you think of a hard choice you've had to make recently?
2. Does God care about our friendships?
3. How can we learn to make wise choices?

Write a Family Prayer

_____

_____

_____

6

▶▶▶▶▶▶▶▶▶▶▶▶▶▶▶▶▶▶▶▶▶▶▶▶▶▶▶▶▶▶▶

THE PLAIN
GRAY DRESS

Linda knelt on the velvety tan couch, staring out the front window and eagerly waiting for the mailman to arrive. She'd seen him stroll past a neighbor's house, carrying a long brown package. *Could it be addressed to me?* she wondered. *Could it be a birthday present?*

Soon there was a knock at the door. Linda ran to open it.

"Package for Miss Linda Walters," announced the tall, lanky mailman.

Linda grabbed the featherweight brown package. "It's my birthday!" she sputtered. Hurrying back into the house, she called over her shoulder, "Thank you!"

Paper and string landed on the floor as Linda tore open her package. "Oh, Mother, look . . . " But Linda's excitement vanished as soon as she pulled away the white tissue paper inside the box.

"Oh, what a pretty dress," said Mother. "It will look lovely with your hazel eyes, Linda. Aunt Janice has such good taste."

"*Lovely*?" grumbled Linda. "A plain old gray dress that I'll never ever wear? It's awful."

"Linda . . . " Mother sighed. "It's *supposed* to be plain. That way we'll have the fun of fixing it up. Now, since pink is your favorite color, I think I have just the thing to make this a perfect 'Linda-dress.' "

Linda watched her mother take a pastel pink ribbon from her sewing cabinet. "You know," Mother said, snipping the ribbon here and there, "sometimes we forget to appreciate the plain, ordinary things in life." Linda watched as her mother wrapped the ribbon around the waist of the gray dress.

"How do you like it now?" asked Mother, standing back to admire her handiwork. "This ribbon makes a perfect sash, doesn't it?" With a few quick twists, she transformed a length of leftover ribbon into a matching hair bow.

Linda tried on her new birthday dress. "It's decorated just right," she admitted. She twirled in front of the mirror three times then stopped abruptly. "I have a question, though," she said, biting her lip. "Do I have to tell Aunt Janice that I *love* it, or can I just say it looks pretty with pink?"

Come and see what God has done, how awesome his works in man's behalf!

Psalm 66:5

▸▸▸▸▸▸▸▸▸▸▸▸▸

Something to Remember
God decorates my life with joy.

Questions for Family Discussion

1. Have you ever expected something exciting but ended up disappointed instead?
2. Can you imagine how Aunt Janice felt as she wrapped Linda's birthday gift?
3. Has God decorated your life with any surprises?
4. Can you think of a nice way to surprise someone this week?

Write a Family Prayer

_____

_____

_____

_____

7

▶▶▶▶▶▶▶▶▶▶▶▶▶▶▶▶▶▶▶▶▶▶▶▶

THE BALANCING SECRET

Jeremy watched excitedly as he sat beside his grandpa on the front row in the big circus tent. The lion tamer, acrobats, and trapeze artists all delighted him. And Jeremy thought he would never stop laughing at the clowns' silly tricks.

Then the tanned, muscular tightrope walker took his place on the platform high above them. As the drumroll began and spotlights criss-crossed the huge circus tent, the performer start-ed across the thin wire, balancing a long pole.

Jeremy covered his eyes. "Is he still up there, Grandpa?" he asked after a few minutes. "Has he fallen yet?"

Grandpa pulled Jeremy's hands away. "See for yourself." He chuckled.

The tightrope walker was still easing across the wire, holding his pole. The crowd grew so quiet that Jeremy could even hear Grandpa's breathing.

"He sure makes it look easy, doesn't he, Grandpa?" whispered Jeremy.

THE BALANCING SECRET

Grandpa nodded. "That's because he pays attention to every little detail."

Later, at their favorite hamburger place, Grandpa explained what he meant by that. "The circus performer has to hold that pole in just the right spot. Otherwise, he would lose his balance and fall."

"Really?" Jeremy asked.

Grandpa's eyes narrowed the way they always did when he had something important to say. "God gave you and me a special part that helps us keep our balance, too. Can you guess what it is?"

"A neck?" asked Jeremy.

"No, try again." Grandpa took a sip of root beer.

"Big feet?"

Grandpa grinned. "You're getting closer."

"Uh . . . strong ankles?" Jeremy bit into his hamburger.

"Big toes," Grandpa finally told him. "God gave us big toes so we wouldn't stumble around like toddlers all our lives. Our big toes keep us steady when we walk."

"Hey, that's cool!" Jeremy laughed. "I guess I never realized how important such little things could be. Oh, by the way, Grandpa, could I have some more fries?"

> Great are the works of the
> LORD; they are pondered by all
> who delight in them.
>
> Psalm 111:2

Kwitcherbellyakin

▶▶▶▶▶▶▶▶▶▶▶▶▶▶

Something to Remember
God thinks of every detail.

Questions for Family Discussion
1. Have you ever wondered how tightrope walkers keep from falling?
2. What would your life be like if God hadn't given you two big toes?
3. Have you ever taken time to thank God for giving you such a wonderful body?

Write a Family Prayer

_____

_____

_____

_____

8

▶▶▶▶▶▶▶▶▶▶▶▶▶▶▶▶▶▶▶▶▶▶▶▶▶▶▶▶▶▶▶▶

THE IDEA GARDEN

Jason's next-door neighbor Bobby began acting strangely. He didn't feel like playing ball or trading baseball cards. He didn't even feel like talking in the backyard after supper.

Jason was puzzled. Was it something he had said? Had he hurt Bobby's feelings or made him angry somehow? "What's wrong, Bobby?" Jason finally asked. "Are you mad at me?"

"Nope," Bobby answered quietly.

"Are you sick?" Jason persisted.

"Nothing's wrong with me," said Bobby. "It's just that my dad lost his job yesterday."

"But how could he lose his job?" asked Jason. "Did he forget to go to work?"

"No," said Bobby, rolling his eyes. "There were too many people working at the factory, and they made some of them quit."

Jason wanted to ask a lot of questions, like, *How will you buy food? Will you have to move away? Will your dad ever find another job?* But the look on Bobby's face told Jason that his friend

didn't feel like answering questions. So Jason just whispered, "Sorry, Bobby." He thought a moment, then added, "It'll work out. You'll see."

"Maybe." Bobby's shaky voice sounded unsure.

That night as Jason lay in bed, an idea popped into his head. A couple of months earlier, he'd helped Mom and Dad plant their summer garden. Many of the tomatoes were already ripe, and the cucumbers would be ready to pick soon—maybe even this coming weekend.

He ran to tell Mom and Dad his idea. "If we leave a bag of garden vegetables on their doorstep every week, they won't have to worry about buying as much food," he said.

"Great idea, son," agreed Dad. "Now I know

THE IDEA GARDEN   **33**

why we planted so many extra tomatoes this year."

Jason was glad that he had talked to Bobby. But he was even happier that God had planted an idea in his mind—an idea that grew and ripened, just like their garden—to help a good friend.

> He who is kind to the poor
> lends to the LORD, and he will
> reward him for what he has
> done.
>
> Proverbs 19:17

▸▸▸▸▸▸▸▸▸▸▸▸▸

Something to Remember

God gave me a heart to serve Him.

Questions for Family Discussion

1. Can you think of a friend or neighbor who has a problem? How could you help that person?
2. What can we do if a person won't accept our help?
3. In what ways can you serve God?

Write a Family Prayer

_____

_____

_____

_____

Kwitcherbellyakin

9

▸▸▸▸▸▸▸▸▸▸▸▸▸▸▸▸▸▸▸▸▸▸▸▸▸▸▸▸▸▸▸▸▸▸▸▸▸

THE GRUMPY NEIGHBOR

Molly headed across the street one summer afternoon to get her brother's tricycle out of Mrs. Bradbury's yard.

The older woman sat on her front porch and peered over her gold-rimmed glasses. "Where do you think you are going, young lady?" she snapped.

"I'm just getting my brother's tricycle," answered Molly. "He forgets to bring it home sometimes."

Mrs. Bradbury's expression was as sour as a green apple. "Well, see that he doesn't forget it in *my* yard next time!" She sniffed, and Molly wondered what was bothering her.

Walking over to the porch, Molly stood on her tiptoes to peek over the porch rail. She watched as Mrs. Bradbury pulled piles of paper from a tall box and spread them out on a table.

"What are you doing?" Molly asked politely.

"Looking at old photographs, that's all," Mrs. Bradbury said. "Run along."

"Photographs of what?" Molly persisted.

"Babies and friends and things like that. Now *goodbye*."

Molly loved looking through photo albums. "May I see just one?"

Mrs. Bradbury sighed and squirmed uncomfortably in her chair. "All right, but hold the pictures by their edges."

"Oh, I already know that rule," said Molly. She took a seat next to grouchy Mrs. Bradbury. One by one, she studied the pictures. And little by little, she began to realize how long Mrs. Bradbury had lived.

She found photos of babies and brothers and sisters and parents, of vacations and birthdays and Christmases and Easters. "Where do all these people live now?" asked Molly, scrunching her nose. "I mean, do they ever come and visit?"

Mrs. Bradbury coughed. "They're very busy," she said, snatching the pictures from the girl.

"Oh," Molly said. She thought for a few seconds. "Then maybe I should start visiting you. Like every Tuesday?"

"That might be nice," admitted Mrs. Bradbury, "if I'm not too busy."

We love because he first loved us.

1 John 4:19

▶▶▶▶▶▶▶▶▶▶▶▶

Something to Remember

God teaches me ways to love others.

Kwitcherbellyakin

Questions for Family Discussion

1. Do you know anyone like Mrs. Bradbury who is always grumbling and complaining?
2. How would you feel if everybody was too busy to listen to you?
3. How do you think God wants us to treat grumpy people?

Write a Family Prayer

_____

_____

_____

_____

10
▸▸▸▸▸▸▸▸▸▸▸▸▸▸▸▸▸▸▸▸▸▸▸▸▸▸▸▸▸▸▸▸▸▸▸▸▸▸▸

A GREEN
THUMB?

Kurt had a green thumb. He could make anything grow—or so he thought when he agreed to take care of fifteen African violets while his grandparents were away on a vacation.

"Just set them in a warm window," Grandma told him. "Not too sunny and not too shady. And water them only when the soil feels dry."

Kurt checked the violets every day after school. He watered them whenever the soil felt loose and dry. And he made sure his cat, Oliver, didn't take his nap on top of them.

One day, Kurt discovered a purple violet drooping like a tired ballerina. He had watered it, fed it special plant food, and even talked to it. Within two days, though, its broad, velvety leaves had wilted into a hopeless heap in the clay pot. *It's impossible*, he thought.

The next day, one of Grandma's friends stopped Kurt in the grocery store. "Hello, young man," she said, patting him affectionately on the back. "How are your grandmother's plants doing?"

Kurt hesitated. "Well, the score is fourteen to one," he admitted. "One of them died."

"Oh, what a shame," the lady replied. "Those violets can be touchy sometimes, just like us. They need a lot of tender, loving care."

The following Tuesday, when Kurt checked Grandma's plants, he noticed something unusual. The droopy violet at the back had perked up. In fact, five tiny buds reached toward the sunshine like hungry baby birds.

"Grandma's friend was right," he said to himself. "All they need is tender, loving care." He moved the plant in front of the others, where it would get more light.

By the time Grandma and Grandpa arrived home, the plant that had looked so sick was blooming with five healthy, purple blossoms. "Looks like you took good care of my violets, Kurtis," observed Grandma. "You must have inherited my green thumb."

Kurt just grinned.

> **"Nothing is impossible with God."**
>
> Luke 1:37

▶▶▶▶▶▶▶▶▶▶▶▶▶▶▶

Something to Remember

God makes anything possible.

Questions for Family Discussion

1. Do you have a green thumb?
2. How do you think Kurt felt when he spotted the five tiny buds on Grandma's violet?
3. Is anything too hard for God?

Write a Family Prayer

_____

_____

_____

_____

11

>>>

THE PEST

Danny stepped out the front door to go for a bike ride. "Oh, no, there he is again," he whispered to himself. "I'm going back inside."

Danny's neighbor, freckle-faced Matt, headed for their house. Matt was different from anyone Danny had ever known. Obnoxious and loud, Matt seemed to bump into trouble wherever he went.

Danny rushed into the house just in time. He hopped onto the flowered sofa and peeked through the living room curtains. *I wonder what he'll do this time,* thought Danny.

"Daniel James, who are you spying on?" Mom laughed. "Let's open those curtains and get some sunlight in here."

"But Matt's coming, and I don't want to talk to him," explained Danny. He reminded Mom of the time Matt dumped Danny's bike in the middle of the street and walked away. "And don't forget my model plane." Danny scowled, remembering how Matt had crushed it.

"Well, I was just going to invite Matt in for

some brownies," Mother told him. "He's alone most of the day, and I thought it would be a nice treat for him."

"Matt doesn't like brownies," Danny lied.

Mother folded her arms and studied her son's face. "Daniel, aren't you glad God has a different view than yours?" she asked.

Danny wrinkled his nose. "What do you mean?"

His mother gently pulled him down next to her on the sofa and looked into his blue eyes. "God loves us so much that He sees right past our shortcomings," she said. "Sometimes we don't know what has happened in a person's life to make them do what they do. But God does. He accepts each of us just as we are. And He is able to turn each one of us into someone wonderful if we'll let Him."

"Even Matt?" asked Danny, rolling his eyes.

"Even Matt," Mother replied. "Now, how about some brownies for the two of you?"

"OK," Danny gave in. "Just make sure you use dishes that won't break."

> From his dwelling place [the Lord] watches all who live on earth—he who forms the hearts of all, who considers everything they do.
>
> Psalm 33:14—15

▶▶▶▶▶▶▶▶▶▶▶▶▶

Something to Remember
God's view is always clearer than mine.

Questions for Family Discussion

1. Do you know anyone like Matt?
2. Does God ever play favorites?
3. How could you help a friend like Matt?

Write a Family Prayer

12

SECOND BEST

Trudy knew how good it felt to work hard and win. She had won spelling bees, art contests, and running races. The bulletin board in her room overflowed with colorful ribbons.

One spring, though, Trudy met her match when a new girl with long legs and an I-can-do-anything attitude arrived at school.

Jealous of Cindi's confidence, Trudy decided to challenge her to a race. "I bet I can beat you around the track Friday at Sports Day," she bragged.

Cindi just snickered. "We'll have to see."

On Friday the whole school met outside for relays, a three-legged race, and wheelbarrow runs. Soon the time came for the biggest event of the day. Students lined both sides of the track, cheering for their favorite runner.

When the starting whistle sounded, Trudy took off like a wild stallion. Within seconds, though, Cindi's long legs carried her right past Trudy. She made the race look easy.

"The winner—Cindi Davis!" cried the announcer.

Trudy's heart sank. She could hardly stand to look at Cindi. But a tap on her shoulder forced her to face her speedier opponent.

"You're good," admitted Cindi, who was still huffing and puffing. "I see why you've won every year."

Trudy managed a weak smile. "I guess I lost this time around, though."

"You didn't lose, silly." Cindi punched Trudy's arm playfully. "You just came in second best."

Trudy thought about it for a moment. *Second best isn't so bad.* "Congratulations, Cindi," she said loud enough for the other kids to hear. Then, with a mischievous smile, she added, "But you'd better watch out next year."

> **Each one should test his own actions. Then he can take pride in himself, without comparing himself to somebody else.**
>
> Galatians 6:4

»»»»»»»»»»»

Something to Remember

God sees me as a winner when I use the talents He has given me.

Questions for Family Discussion

1. Have you ever worked hard to win a special award?
2. How do you feel when someone is faster or smarter or more popular than you?
3. Does God think of us as winners and losers?

Write a Family Prayer

_____

_____

_____

_____

Kwitcherbellyakin

13

▶▶▶▶▶▶▶▶▶▶▶▶▶▶▶▶▶▶▶▶▶▶▶▶▶▶▶▶▶▶▶▶▶▶▶▶

CHICKEN SOUP
TO THE RESCUE

Every year during Thanksgiving vacation, Charlie and his dad would pack fishing gear, bed rolls, and an ice chest full of goodies. For three days they would camp in a tiny trailer near Lake Morrow, fishing all day and sitting around a toasty fire until late at night.

But this year, disaster struck. The packed ice chest sat waiting by the kitchen door, and the trailer sagged under the weight of suitcases, fishing gear, and sleeping bags. Charlie's warm winter jacket and heavy socks lay draped over a chair next to his bed, ready to go. Everything was set, except Charlie. He felt too weak even to crawl out of bed.

"Here," said Mom, popping a thermometer into his mouth. She waited three minutes then winced. "Ugh," she said, feeling Charlie's forehead again. "One hundred and two."

Dad flashed Charlie his most sympathetic look. "Sorry, partner," he said sadly. "Looks like we'll have to delay our trip until spring."

Word of Charlie's illness spread around the neighborhood. One of his buddies, Steve, telephoned him and said, "If you're too sick to fish, you must be *really* sick!"

Around noon, Steve and another friend, Gary, decided to take action. Browsing through some old magazines, they cut out every fish picture they could find. A heavy piece of brown wrapping paper, measured to fit a serving tray, became a "fishy" place mat. Then Gary printed fish jokes all over a big paper cup.

Steve filled a bowl with hot chicken noodle soup. "Okay, we're all set," he said, grabbing a box of fish-shaped crackers.

He and Gary crossed the street and rang the doorbell. When Charlie's dad answered the door, the boys handed him the tray.

"Tell Charlie that he'll probably catch more fish on his tray than he would've at the lake, anyway," Gary teased.

Charlie's dad thanked the boys and closed the door. "Hey, Charlie," he called, "a couple of fishy-looking characters brought you a special lunch!"

Charlie laughed when he saw the tray. "I think those fishy-looking characters are really good friends," he said.

> **All of you, live in harmony**
> **with one another; be**
> **sympathetic, love as brothers,**
> **be compassionate and humble.**
>
> 1 Peter 3:8

Kwitcherbellyakin

▶▶▶▶▶▶▶▶▶▶▶▶▶▶

Something to Remember

God shows His love through
caring friends.

Questions for Family Discussion

1. Have you ever planned to go somewhere special but ended up sick in bed?
2. What are some ways you could help a friend who is not feeling well?
3. How does God bless you through friendships?

Write a Family Prayer

_____

_____

_____

_____

14

▶▶▶▶▶▶▶▶▶▶▶▶▶▶▶▶▶▶▶▶▶▶▶▶▶▶▶▶▶▶

NOBODY NOTICED

As Lynn strolled through a toy store in the mall, she met a white-haired woman carrying a shiny yellow shopping bag.

"Can you help me, dear?" the stranger asked.

Lynn knew just what to do. First she called her mother, who was standing at the other end of the aisle.

"This is my mom," said Lynn. The two women shook hands. "Mama, she needs help," whispered Lynn.

"I'm a little embarrassed," explained the other lady. "I think I'm lost. You see, I'm supposed to meet my daughter in front of Furhman's Jewelers, but I can't find a store by that name."

Lynn tapped her mother's arm. "I know where that store is. May I take her there?"

"Why don't the three of us walk there together?" suggested Mama.

So Lynn, Mama, and the white-haired woman made their way through the crowded mall, chatting like old friends. Nobody noticed an embar-

Kwitcherbellyakin

rassed old woman in need or a girl and her mother who were guiding her to Furhman's Jewelers. And nobody noticed how happy it made Lynn feel to help a stranger.

Around the corner from a flower shop, next to a bubbling fountain, a woman in a red jacket stood waiting in the doorway of Furhman's Jewelers. "Oh, there you are, Mom," she said, checking her watch. "I was beginning to think you were lost or something." She hugged her mother.

"Ha!" The older lady winked at Lynn. "Lost? Why, I've just been visiting with some friends."

After exchanging good-byes, Lynn turned to Mama. "Why did that lady pick *me* to help her?"

NOBODY NOTICED

Mama wrapped her arm around Lynn's waist. "God must have noticed what a helpful and willing heart you have," she said. "He led her right to you."

Lynn smiled inside. *Then I hope God also notices how hungry I am for an ice cream.*

> **Do not withhold good from those who deserve it, when it is in your power to act.**
>
> Proverbs 3:27

▸▸▸▸▸▸▸▸▸▸▸▸▸▸▸

Something to Remember

God remembers every good deed.

Questions for Family Discussion

1. What should you do if a stranger asks directions?
2. Is your heart helpful and willing to serve God?
3. How can you tell when God has a special job for you?

Write a Family Prayer

_____

_____

_____

_____

15

>>>

THE WRONG
SHADE OF BLUE

Brett and his sister, Heather, wanted to make a surprise gift for their Uncle Joe's birthday. "Let's paint a picture for his cabin," suggested Brett. "He could hang it in that empty spot over the fireplace."

Uncle Joe spent most of his spare time at his lakeside cabin. Brett and Heather liked to fish with him off the long dock that hugged his property. They decided to paint a picture of that dock and the lake. Gathering together their paints and a new canvas they bought from the art store, Brett and Heather spread newspaper on the kitchen table. Then they borrowed a couple of Dad's old T-shirts to protect their clothes.

"You paint the dock, and I'll do the sky," suggested Heather.

"Good idea," Brett said. "Then we'll both paint the water part."

Brett and Heather painted every day after school. At the end of the week, Brett's dock looked almost real enough to stand on. Heather's sky swirled with wind-tossed clouds.

When it came time to paint the water, though, Heather hesitated. "Which blue should we use," she asked her brother, "deep blue or this lighter one?"

"The darker shade," said Brett.

Working together, Heather and Brett filled the empty spaces around the dock with brush strokes of cool lake water. Heather twirled her paintbrush to create tiny ripples on the canvas.

Brett carefully blended the line where the lake met the sky then stood back for a better look. "Oh, no," he moaned. "The water looks cold and stormy. I think we've used the wrong shade of blue."

"I don't think so." Heather shrugged. "The color I used for the sky makes it look like it's starting to get dark out. And Uncle Joe likes to fish at night when the water looks like this. I think he'll like it because he catches his biggest fish at night."

Heather added a small wave slapping against the dock. "Besides," she reasoned, "we're just the artists. God's the one who made the water that color. The lake has so many colors at different times, I don't think we could have chosen a wrong shade."

Brett cocked his head and looked at the painting again. "Maybe you're right," he said with a smile. "I think Uncle Joe is going to like this painting!"

**The heavens are yours, and
yours also the earth; you [God]
founded the world and all that
is in it.**

Psalm 89:11

▶▶▶▶▶▶▶▶▶▶▶▶▶▶▶

Something to Remember

God brightens my world with colors.

Questions for Family Discussion

1. Do you like to paint? Have you ever painted a
   picture for someone you love?
2. What would our world be like without colors?
2. Why do you think God gave us colors?

Write a Family Prayer

_____

_____

_____

_____

16
>>>

COOLING OFF

Elaine and her friends Joan and Brenda decided to go on a long summer bike outing one day. "My grandfather's farm has all kinds of cool, shady bike trails," said Elaine. "We can ride there and have a picnic at his pond."

Dark-eyed Brenda nodded enthusiastically. "That sounds like fun," she said. "What are we waiting for?"

The three friends each packed a lunch and tucked some extra goodies in their bike bags to share. Then they met at an intersection in the country. "It's a perfect day for biking," said Joan. "Cool and breezy."

By late morning, though, all three were complaining.

"Whose idea was this, anyway?" muttered Brenda. "It's hot enough to cook an egg on my forehead."

"Yeah, I feel like a baked potato," moaned Elaine.

Brenda gave Elaine a sarcastic look. "I

thought your grandfather's farm had cool, shady bike trails. You call this road cool and shady?"

"Let's ride over to Grandpa's house," Elaine suggested. "We can cool off there for a while."

The girls pedaled as fast as they could, weaving around clumps of trees and old rusty farm equipment.

"I'd love to run into a gigantic block of ice," said Joan. "I think I'd sit on it."

"Well, I'd probably hug it," hollered Brenda, leading the way up a grassy knoll.

When the girls reached Grandpa's red farmhouse, Elaine pointed to the hose hanging on the side of the house. The girls dumped their bikes and raced over to the water hose.

All three pushed and shoved to be the first to get some water. Then they fussed at each other about how long each took for her drink. None of them even noticed Grandpa standing off to the side, grinning at them.

Grandpa strolled over to them and pointed to the hose. "Jesus gives us an even better kind of water," he told the girls.

"Aw, Grandpa," Elaine said, "all three of us are already Christians, if that's what you mean."

"Well, that hose may cool off your bodies, but how about your tempers?" Grandpa asked. "Any chance Jesus' water of life can make a difference there?"

"Whoever drinks the water I
give him will never thirst.
Indeed, the water I give him
will become in him a spring of
water welling up to eternal
life."

John 4:14

▶▶▶▶▶▶▶▶▶▶▶▶▶▶

Something to Remember

God can make a difference
in the way I act.

Questions for Family Discussion

1. What do you think the girls need to do to cool
   their tempers?
2. How can having Jesus in your life make a
   difference in the way you act?
3. Have you accepted Jesus and His living water
   that Grandpa talked about?

Write a Family Prayer

_____

_____

_____

_____

17
ONLY A HILL

Luis loved summer camp—except for one thing. The campground lay at the bottom of a big mountain everyone called Ol' Smokey, and one day each year, the campers had to climb that mountain! Luis trembled at the thought of it. This year, Luis was so afraid of climbing the mountain that he almost didn't go to camp, but a friend talked him into going anyway.

Then, halfway through the week, the camp director, Mr. Rollins, stood after dinner to make a special announcement. "Campers," he said in his clear, deep voice, "tomorrow's the big day. We're going to capture Ol' Smokey!"

All the kids sprang to their feet, cheering wildly and slapping each other on the back. Luis hooted and hollered, too, pretending to be thrilled about the hike. But inside, his stomach churned.

Mr. Rollins quieted the campers. "We'll meet at the flagpole at seven o'clock sharp," he reminded everyone. "Don't be late."

As boys and girls filed out of the cafeteria, Luis overheard their excited chatter.

"This'll be my third year in a row," boasted one.

"Last year I got to plant the camp flag at the top," bragged another.

Luis didn't dare say a word for fear of giving away his secret. No one must know how his knees shook just thinking about first having to cross the icy creek at the base of Ol' Smokey. Luis's head spun as he remembered the narrow, unsteady log that served as a bridge. And then there was the huge mountain with its steep, slippery trails!

As Luis headed out to the ball field, Mr. Rollins slapped him affectionately on the back. "Ready for the big hike?" he asked.

"Uh . . . not really," stammered Luis. "I mean, sort of."

Mr. Rollins smiled. "Not crazy about being up there so high, huh, Luis?"

How does he know? Luis wondered.

"I used to hate it, too," Mr. Rollins confided. He glanced around to make sure no one else was listening. "But you know what? One year God gave me a great idea. Now I don't think about how high the mountain is. I just pretend it's a little hill."

"But what about crossing the creek?" whispered Luis.

"Just look ahead instead of down," suggested Mr. Rollins. "That's what I do. Think about one step at a time, and you'll do fine."

Luis still wasn't convinced. "But what about . . . ?"

Kwitcherbellyakin

**Cast all your anxiety on him
because he cares for you.**

1 Peter 5:7

▸▸▸▸▸▸▸▸▸▸▸▸▸▸▸▸

Something to Remember

God helps me overcome fear.

Questions for Family Discussion

1. Can you think of one thing that frightens you?
2. Do you know anyone like Mr. Rollins, who gives you helpful advice?
3. What would happen if you avoided every new experience that scared you?
4. Can you remember a time when God calmed your fears?

Write a Family Prayer

_____

_____

_____

_____

18

▸▸▸▸▸▸▸▸▸▸▸▸▸▸▸▸▸▸▸▸▸▸▸▸▸▸▸▸▸▸▸▸▸

ANOTHER CHANCE

One Friday after school, Glenda packed her overnight bag, pillow, and sleeping bag for a sleepover at her best friend's house.

When Dad got home from work, he dropped Glenda off at Marlene's. "Have a good time," he said.

Glenda and Marlene played table games, then shared a jumbo bowl of popcorn as they watched their favorite shows on TV and talked and giggled late into the night.

As they talked about some of their friends at school, Glenda remembered something. "Hey, Marlene," she said, "I need to tell you something, but you have to promise not to get mad."

Marlene sat straight up in her sleeping bag on the floor. "What is it?"

"Well, remember that science book you borrowed from Lori? She says that she's in big trouble because you lost it."

"Wha-a-at?" squealed Marlene. "Lori's lying! I never even borrowed a book from her."

Kwitcherbellyakin

"Well, that's what she told all the kids. And her mother says you'd better find the book, or else!"

Marlene was furious. "Some friend Lori turned out to be!" she fumed. "First she makes up a story. Then she blabs to the whole school."

Glenda wished she had kept her mouth shut. "Why don't we phone Lori tomorrow morning?" she suggested. "Maybe this was all a big mistake. She at least deserves a chance to explain."

"Anybody who tells a lie like that doesn't deserve another chance," snapped Marlene.

Now Glenda wished she had never mentioned it in the first place. *How can I get Marlene to give Lori another chance?* she wondered.

> **Be kind and compassionate to one another, forgiving each other, just as in Christ God forgave you.**
>
> Ephesians 4:32

▶▶▶▶▶▶▶▶▶▶▶▶▶

Something to Remember

God never gives up on me.

Questions for Family Discussion

1. Have you ever been blamed for something you didn't do?
2. Can you remember a time when you falsely accused someone?

ANOTHER CHANCE

3. How *might* Glenda convince Marlene to give Lori another chance?
4. Why is it important for us to forgive others when they hurt or disappoint us?

Write a Family Prayer

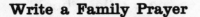

_____

_____

_____

_____

19

►►►

MAXINE THE WONDER DOG

Pamela didn't have a pet until a little puppy, half starved and whimpering, wandered into her yard one rainy afternoon. Pam found her shivering near the back gate.

"No name, huh?" asked Pamela, checking the pup for tags. "Well, then, what am I supposed to call you?"

The pup stared up at Pam with sad, unblinking eyes.

Pamela reached out to pet her, but the pup jumped away. "Why are you so scared, puppy?" whispered Pamela. "Don't you have a home? Doesn't anybody love you?"

Pam continued talking to the frightened puppy, and little by little, the pup began to relax at the sound of her voice. She even followed Pam up onto the back steps and just sat there. Pam quickly ran inside and returned seconds later with a small white bowl. "Have some milk," she coaxed, setting it next to the puppy. "It'll warm you up." Within seconds, the bowl was empty.

When Pamela opened the door to get more, in one quick burst, the mysterious pup raced inside.

"Wait!" shrieked Pamela. "You can't go in there."

The now-frisky pup bounded up the stairs, straight to Pamela's room, where she hid in a far corner under the bed. *Great! Now I'll never get her out of there!*

Pamela began calling out all the dog names she could think of. "Arnie, Fido, Chomper, Tiny, Blacky . . . " The list went on and on. "Peanuts, Tippy, Bernard, Maxine . . . "

Suddenly the pup flew out from under the bed with a yelp.

"Maxine?" repeated Pamela. "Is your name 'Maxine'?" The silly pup barked until she was breathless, running in circles every time Pamela called her name.

Pamela scooped the pup into her arms and looked into eyes now sparkling with happiness. "I wonder where you came from," said Pam, "and I wonder how I'll help you find your way home again."

A wet kiss on the nose made Pamela giggle. "For now, I'll call you Maxine the Wonder Dog," she said. "How's that for starters?"

Maxine barked her approval, and her wagging tail sent its own message: *And for now I'll call this Home,* she seemed to say. *How's that for starters?*

How many are your works, O
LORD! In wisdom you made
them all; the earth is full of
your creatures.

Psalm 104:24

▶▶▶▶▶▶▶▶▶▶▶▶▶▶

Something to Remember

God created animals for me to enjoy.

Questions for Family Discussion

1. Do you have a pet?
2. Why do you think God created so many different kinds of animals?
3. Have you ever felt lost and alone like Maxine
   did?

Write a Family Prayer

_____

_____

_____

_____

20

>>>>>>>>>>>>>>>>>>>>>>>>>>>>>>>>>>>>>>>

KATIE'S
CHRISTMAS COLD

On Christmas Eve, Katie and her sister, Ellen, were helping Mommy bake cookies.

"Mmm-mm!" cried Ellen. "Everything smells like Christmas! Don't you just love that sweet cinnamony smell, Katie?"

Katie sniffed the air. "I don't smell anything," she complained. "How come I don't smell anything?" Before she could say another word, she sneezed three times.

"Katie Marie," said Mommy, "it sounds like you've gotten yourself a cold for Christmas." Mommy went to the refrigerator and poured a tall glass of orange juice. "Here," she said. "Drink this juice. It'll be good for you."

Ellen sneaked a ball of sugar-cookie dough. "Yummy, yummy!" she whispered.

Katie popped a piece of the sticky dough in her mouth, too, but made a sour face. "Tastes like . . . mush," she complained.

Mom went out to the living room to talk to

Dad. "Poor thing," she said. "Katie can't smell or taste. What an awful time of year to have a cold."

Dad stepped into the warm kitchen and sat down at the table. He pulled Katie onto his lap. "Sounds like your taste buds have gone on the blink," he said. "But have you ever thought about what it would be like if God hadn't given us those little red bumps on our tongue?"

"Icky," decided Katie. "That's what it'd be like."

Dad pointed to his Bible, which sat on a shelf nearby. "Scripture talks about a man named King David, who said that he could 'taste' God's words. Imagine that!"

"What did they taste like?" Katie asked.

"Well, David said that God's words were 'sweeter than honey.'"

Katie's sister started to giggle. "Why would God's words taste like honey? And how could that king guy eat them, anyway?"

Katie began to laugh along with Ellen. "Yeah, Dad," she said. "That sounds crazy." Dad ran his fingers through his hair and smiled. "Well, God's words are the rules we are to live by. They're good rules because He loves us."

"But how can we taste them?" Katie and Ellen asked together.

"By thinking about them and then obeying them," said Dad, "our lives will 'taste' sweeter."

"As sweet as cookie dough?" wondered Ellen.

"Even sweeter." Dad winked.

How sweet are your words to
my taste, sweeter than honey
to my mouth!

Psalm 119:103

▶▶▶▶▶▶▶▶▶▶▶▶▶▶

Something to Remember

God gives me two ways to taste.

Questions for Family Discussion

1. Do you ever help bake cookies at your house?
2. Where can we go to "taste" some of God's words?
3. How do you feel about the rules God has given us?

Write a Family Prayer

_____

_____

_____

_____

Kwitcherbellyakin

21

>>>

THE MISSING KEY

Jody always wore a pink satin ribbon around her neck. On that ribbon hung a tiny gold key that fit into the lock of a beautiful musical jewelry box her grandmother had given her for Christmas.

"Be careful with the key," cautioned Grandma. "It's small and you could easily misplace it."

Jody decided that the best way to keep it was to wear it wherever she went. She wore the key to school, church, and even on overnight trips to friends' houses.

But something terrible happened one night while she slept over at Marilyn's house. Her key disappeared! "I remember having it while we were playing tag," Jody recalled.

"And I saw it dangling from your neck while we watched TV," Marilyn remembered.

Jody and Marilyn searched everywhere, from the upstairs bathroom to the basement game closet. But by nine o'clock, they still hadn't found the missing key.

Marilyn sighed. "Well, at least God knows where it is," she said. "Maybe we should ask Him where to look."

Jody roared with laughter. "Oh, sure, Marilyn," she teased. "And I suppose a big finger will point right to the missing key."

Marilyn's face reddened. "Well, just wait and see, Jody," she insisted. "God will find your key."

The next morning Jody awoke, feeling something wet and cold pressed against her arm. "Bowser!" She gave Marilyn's shaggy dog a push. "Go away and let me sleep."

Kwitcherbellyakin

But Bowser wouldn't budge.

Jody leaned over the edge of the bed to investigate. There, connecting poor Bowser to the bedpost in a tangled mess, was a pink satin ribbon with a shiny key on the end. Jody shook Marilyn awake. "You're not going to believe this," she told her friend. "God *did* find my key! And look who He sent to deliver it!"

> Devote yourselves to prayer,
> being watchful and thankful.
>
> Colossians 4:2

▸▸▸▸▸▸▸▸▸▸▸▸▸▸

Something to Remember

God sees everything I lose.

Questions for Family Discussion

1. Do you know how it feels to lose something precious?
2. What's the first thing you should do when you lose something?
3. Did God know where Jody's key was the whole time?
4. Could God ever lose His love for us?

Write a Family Prayer

_____

_____

_____

THE MISSING KEY 73

22

▶▶▶▶▶▶▶▶▶▶▶▶▶▶▶▶▶▶▶▶▶▶▶▶▶▶▶▶▶▶▶▶▶▶▶▶

TRADING PLACES

Ben was the envy of his schoolmates. He lived in a gigantic house at the edge of the clear blue lake. Every morning his dad drove him to school in a little red sports car.

"Riding the bus is stupid," Ben taunted the other kids.

Ryan sighed every time he saw Ben climb out of the little red sports car. "I'd like to be in his shoes for a day, just to see what 'rich' feels like," he said one day.

"Yeah," agreed Tim. "He probably has a maid who ties his shoes for him."

"And a butler who brings popcorn to his room on a silver tray," added Ryan.

One day after Thanksgiving break, Ben returned to school and bragged, "I spent five days visiting my uncle in London."

"Ben has it made!" whispered Tim.

"He's spoiled rotten," said Ryan.

But when March rolled around, Ben suddenly missed three days of school in a row.

"Where have you been?" Ryan asked when

Ben finally returned to class. "You been sick or what?"

"No!" snapped Ben. "Does it look like I've been sick? I'm getting ready to move to London, that's all."

"That's *all?*" echoed Ryan. "But why do you have to move?"

"My parents want me to see what another country is like," explained Ben. "I'll even have to go to school in the summertime."

"Oh." Ryan suddenly felt sad for Ben.

Tim lowered his eyes. "Sorry you're leaving," he said quietly.

They watched Ben walk away. "I'm glad I'm not in his shoes," decided Ryan.

"Me, too," agreed Tim. "I guess I like it right where I am."

> **The blessing of the Lord brings wealth, and he adds no trouble to it.**
>
> Proverbs 10:22

▶▶▶▶▶▶▶▶▶▶▶▶▶▶

Something to Remember

God never makes mistakes.

Questions for Family Discussion

1. Have you ever daydreamed about trading places with someone?
2. Why did Ben's schoolmates envy him?

TRADING PLACES 75

3. When God promises wealth, what does he mean?
4. Can you think of four things that money can't buy?

Write a Family Prayer

_____

_____

_____

_____

23

▶▶▶▶▶▶▶▶▶▶▶▶▶▶▶▶▶▶▶▶▶▶▶▶▶▶▶▶▶▶▶

LATASHA'S SCRAPBOOK

Grandparent's Day was only a week away, and Latasha could hardly wait to tell Mom and Dad about her plan. "I thought of it right in the middle of Sunday school," she confessed when they got home from church. She ran past them into the house, calling, "Wait right there."

Seconds later, she returned from her room with a shoe box. "This is everything I've kept since I was little," she said, pulling the lid off the box. "It's stuff that reminds me of Grandpa and Grandma."

Mom grinned at Dad and they both took a seat on the sofa next to their daughter.

"Oh, look," said Latasha, dumping the contents on the coffee table. "Here's a ticket from the amusement park." She smiled as she recalled her day with Grandma and Grandpa. "Grandma had a clown sing 'Happy Birthday' to me."

"What's this scrap of gingham?" wondered Mom.

"Oh, that's from a quilt that Grandma and I

made. It's on the bed in her guest room, where I sleep. Grandpa took a picture of us working on it." She handed Dad a snapshot. "I helped with that part," she said, pointing to a grouping of red and blue squares, "and Grandma finished the rest."

"It's beautiful," said Dad.

Latasha and her parents spent nearly an hour rummaging through the boxful of memories. They found old letters, cards, and crackly autumn leaves from a chilly outing with her grandparents in the park.

"I want to surprise Grandma and Grandpa by putting everything in a scrapbook for Grandparent's Day," Latasha explained.

Dad smiled broadly. "That's a great idea," he said.

"They'll love it," agreed Mom.

So the next day Latasha bought a bright blue scrapbook at the store. In careful letters, she wrote, *My Memory Book* on the front cover and spent every spare moment she could find pasting all her mementos into it.

When her grandparents arrived on Grandparents Day, the next Sunday, Latasha met them at the door. The three of them sat close together on the sofa and thumbed slowly through her Memory Book.

"Oh, it's wonderful, Latasha!" Grandma exclaimed. "I'll keep it on the coffee table."

Grandpa nodded. "That way we can enjoy it often, and you can look at it every time you visit us. In fact," he said, rubbing his silver mustache, "how about coming this weekend?"

**The memory of the righteous
will be a blessing.**

Proverbs 10:7

▶▶▶▶▶▶▶▶▶▶▶▶▶▶▶

Something to Remember

God gave me my memory.

Questions for Family Discussion

1. Have you ever done something special to honor your grandparents?
2. What are some of your favorite memories?
3. How would your life be different if God hadn't created you with the ability to remember?

Write a Family Prayer

_____

_____

_____

_____

24
▸▸▸▸▸▸▸▸▸▸▸▸▸▸▸▸▸▸▸▸▸▸▸▸▸▸▸▸▸▸▸▸▸▸

PLAYGROUND MISSIONARY

While Teresa was playing tag with friends at the park one day, she saw a freckle-faced girl standing in line at the drinking fountain. Teresa had never seen the girl before.

Teresa walked over to talk to her. "Do you come here very often?" she asked.

"No," the freckle-faced girl answered. Then she looked away quickly.

"I've never seen you before," said Teresa. "Do you live in one of those houses over there?"

"Yep." The freckle-faced girl looked down and fidgeted with a button on her blouse.

"What's your name?" Teresa persisted.

"Deena," the girl muttered.

"Want to play tag with my friends and me?" Teresa asked. "We need one more, and you could be 'It' if you want."

"No," said Deena. "I don't like that game." She twirled on her heels and ran over to the swings without even saying good-bye.

Teresa stared after her. She felt sad and mad

at the same time—sad for Deena because she had no friends but mad because Deena didn't want to play.

One of Teresa's friends whispered something in Teresa's ear.

"That's a good idea," said Teresa. They ran over to the freckle-faced girl. "We're having a Sunday school party tomorrow night," Teresa told her. "Want to come?"

"Yuck!" said Deena. "I don't go to Sunday school."

Teresa refused to give up. "That's okay," she said softly. "You can come to the party anyway. You like cupcakes, don't you?"

Deena thought for a moment. "What kind of cupcakes?" she asked, tipping her head to one side.

"All kinds," said Teresa. "Every kind you can think of."

"Okay," said Deena, turning to leave. "Maybe I'll come."

"It's the red-brick church at the end of the street," Teresa told her. "The one with the mothers carrying plates of cupcakes inside."

"Tell her the rest, silly," said one of the other kids.

"Oh, yeah," remembered Teresa. "It's also a church where you can find out about God."

Love is patient, love is kind.

1 Corinthians 13:4

PLAYGROUND MISSIONARY   **81**

▶▶▶▶▶▶▶▶▶▶▶▶▶

Something to Remember
God can use me as a witness.

Questions for Family Discussion
1. Can you think of someone who's not very friendly?
2. What is the difference between being shy and being unfriendly?
3. How does it make you feel when someone won't return your kindness?
4. Can God use you as a missionary? How?

Write a Family Prayer

_____

_____

_____

_____

Kwitcherbellyakin

25

▶▶▶▶▶▶▶▶▶▶▶▶▶▶▶▶▶▶▶▶▶▶▶▶▶▶▶▶▶▶▶▶▶▶▶▶▶▶

TOO MUCH
TO DO

Betty loved to run errands for Mrs. Duggard, the widow who lived down the street. In fact, the last time she saw her, Betty had promised to help harvest her garden when it was ready.

Early one morning, as Betty headed to a friend's house, she heard someone calling her name.

"Have a moment to spare?" called Mrs. Duggard.

Betty ran up the sidewalk and stepped inside Mrs. Duggard's cool screened porch. "What's new, Mrs. D?" Betty knew the woman liked the nickname Betty had given her.

"Well, dear," began Mrs. Duggard, "my garden is overflowing with tomatoes and beans. I looked for you last Saturday, but you didn't come."

"Are you sure they're ready to pick?" asked Betty.

"They're *begging* us to pick them." Mrs. Duggard laughed. "If we don't get at them today, they'll start rotting."

Betty didn't have the heart to tell the woman that she was on her way to meet a friend. "Sure thing," she said, taking Mrs. Duggard by the hand. "Let's get busy before it starts raining."

After they had finished harvesting the garden, they started back to the house. Suddenly Mrs. Duggard stopped. "Oh, dear, I just remembered something very important," she said. "My little dog, Charlotte, needs her toenails trimmed. Think you could help me hold her?"

"Sure," Betty said reluctantly. She followed Mrs. Duggard into the house.

An unpleasant surprise awaited them when they stepped into the living room. Charlotte, whose favorite doggy game was to toss her rubber ball back and forth, had knocked over a whole row of potted plants.

"Oh, Charlotte!" scolded Mrs. Duggard. "You've really done it this time!"

Betty helped Mrs. Duggard sweep up the dirt and broken pots. Then Betty held Charlotte in her lap while Mrs. Duggard trimmed the dog's toenails with a special clipper.

"Just one more thing," said Mrs. Duggard.

Betty's heart sank. She liked helping Mrs. Duggard, but this was getting ridiculous! "Mrs. D," she said, giving her an exasperated look. "You have too much to do for one day—"

"I know, dear," interrupted Mrs. Duggard. "And I'm so thankful you came along."

Kwitcherbellyakin

It is God who works in you to
will and to act according to
his good purpose.

Philippians 2:13

▶▶▶▶▶▶▶▶▶▶▶▶▶

Something to Remember

God wants me to serve others.

Questions for Family Discussion:

1. Do you ever get tired of helping?
2. Do you think Mrs. Duggard was unfair to Betty?
3. Could Betty have found a way to help Mrs. Duggard and still visit her friend? How?
4. Can you think of someone who has a reputation for being helpful and kind?

Write a Family Prayer

_____

_____

_____

_____

26

▶▶▶▶▶▶▶▶▶▶▶▶▶▶▶▶▶▶▶▶▶▶▶▶▶▶▶▶▶▶▶▶▶▶▶▶

CAMPOUT TROUBLES

Keith and his friends pitched a tent one night in his backyard. They brought a supply of popcorn, cookies, and soft drinks to stash near their sleeping bags.

After trading spooky stories, Keith suggested that they play charades.

"I played that game once and hated it," protested Larry.

"That's a wimpy game for girls," teased Dale.

Keith pouted. "You guys don't know how to have fun," he grumbled. "We might as well go to sleep."

"Wait, I have an idea," said Larry. "Let's get your dad's police radio. We can listen to emergency calls."

"No way!" cried Keith. "Dad would be furious. I can only listen to it when he's around."

"But he *is* around," teased Larry. "He's around the corner, inside the house sleeping."

"Yeah," said Dale. "Besides, we'll be careful. And we can put it back inside before morning."

Keith reluctantly agreed, and he and his friends tiptoed into Dad's study. Keith grabbed the radio and motioned for Larry to carry the long orange extension cord back to the tent.

When Keith turned the radio on, a shrill squeal cut through the night air. Within seconds, his mother was running across the yard in her bathrobe.

She stood outside the tent, hands on hips, giving Keith her Famous Look. "Keith Everett," she scolded, "what would your daddy say about all this?"

"He'd say I'm in big trouble," mumbled Keith.

**Because he himself suffered
when he was tempted, he is
able to help those who are
being tempted.**

Hebrews 2:18

▶▶▶▶▶▶▶▶▶▶▶▶▶▶

Something to Remember

God helps me say no.

Questions for Family Discussion

1. Why is it sometimes hard to say no to good friends?
2. What do you think Keith could have done when Larry and Dale insisted on using Dad's radio?
3. Why is God the best one to turn to when we're tempted?

Write a Family Prayer

_____

_____

_____

_____

27

▶▶▶▶▶▶▶▶▶▶▶▶▶▶▶▶▶▶▶▶▶▶▶▶▶▶▶▶▶▶

EVIE'S SECRET PLACE

Evie had a big problem. She needed to talk to someone about it.

First, she found Mama, who was working at her sewing machine. "Mama, can I talk to you a minute?" asked Evie. "Melissa and I got into a big fight, and—"

Mama waved Evie away. "Not now, honey," she said. "I'm trying to finish these curtains, and I'm having a little trouble with the hem."

Evie hung her head.

"Let's talk later, okay?" asked Mama. She gave Evie a kiss on the cheek and returned to her sewing.

Evie sat on the steps to the upstairs bedrooms. Hot tears stung her eyes as she thought about her friend Melissa being angry with her.

Just then Evie's sister, Carly, came flying down the stairs three at a time. "Watch out!" she called.

Evie tugged at Carly's sweatshirt sleeve. "Can

I talk to you for a minute?" she asked. "It's about Melissa and me."

"Are you guys fighting again?" groaned Carly. "I'm *so* tired of hearing about your stupid arguments."

Evie's lower lip trembled.

"I'm sure it'll work out, Evie," said Carly, patting her on the back. "You and Melissa always end up solving your problems."

Evie climbed the stairs to her room. She felt as if a heavy weight were strapped to her back. *Nobody cares,* she thought, blinking back tears.

Her secret place in the corner by the blue bookcase was bathed in sunlight. Evie kicked off her shoes and grabbed a pillow to hug. There she sat, leaning against the wall near the window.

"Melissa and I had a big fight," she told God, "the kind that makes me feel sick inside." She paused for a deep breath then asked God to forgive her for arguing with her friend. "Could You please fix it for us?" she asked.

> **You are forgiving and good, O Lord, abounding in love to all who call to you.**
>
> Psalm 86:5

▸▸▸▸▸▸▸▸▸▸▸▸▸▸▸

Something to Remember

God is never too busy to listen.

Questions for Family Discussion

1. Do you ever feel that no one listens to you?
2. Do you consider yourself a good listener?
3. Is God a good listener?
4. Do you have a secret place where you go to talk to God?
5. How could Evie make things right with Melissa?

Write a Family Prayer

_____

_____

_____

_____

28

>>>>>>>>>>>>>>>>>>>>>>>>>>>>>>>>>>>>

THE BEST
STORYBOOK

One weekend Grandpa and Grandma invited Karen to stay at their house in the country. "Bring along anything you want," said Grandpa. "But be sure to bring along my favorite storybook."

Karen giggled. She loved to hear Grandpa read from her thick, red book filled with bedtime stories—especially when he made his voice sound like the different characters in the stories.

Karen pulled her brown suitcase from the hall closet. She packed blouses, jeans, underwear, and pajamas.

"Don't forget your toothbrush and a dress for Sunday school," Mama reminded her.

"And my red storybook," added Karen.

That night at her grandparents' house, Karen snuggled beneath a soft, warm blanket with a tulip pattern on it.

Grandpa sat on the edge of her bed, his glasses perched on the end of his nose. "Ready?" he asked Karen.

"Ready," she said, wondering which story he had selected.

Grandpa read the story about a beautiful garden. "I know this part," Karen whispered. "The man's name is Adam and the lady's name is Eve."

Grandpa read to Karen how God let Adam name every single animal.

"Even the *gnu?*" Karen laughed. She always said that.

Grandpa punched her playfully in the arm. "Even the gnu," he said. Then, when he was finished reading, he said with a smile, "Just think, God cares about Karens as much as he does gnus."

Karen smiled back, and Grandpa kissed her good night.

Then Grandma came into the room and gave Karen a hug. "Did you enjoy your story?" she asked.

"It was the best ever," said Karen.

Grandpa set Karen's red Bible on the nightstand. "I'm glad you brought my favorite storybook," he said. "It's like a bedtime snack."

> **All your words are true; all your righteous laws are eternal.**
>
> Psalm 119:160

▶▶▶▶▶▶▶▶▶▶▶▶▶

Something to Remember

God's Word never grows old.

Questions for Family Discussion

1. What was Karen's favorite bedtime storybook?
2. Why did God give us the Bible?
3. Do you know someone who has never read God's Word?
4. Do you have a favorite Bible story?

Write a Family Prayer

_____

_____

_____

_____

Kwitcherbellyakin

29

▶▶▶▶▶▶▶▶▶▶▶▶▶▶▶▶▶▶▶▶▶▶▶▶▶▶▶▶▶▶▶▶▶

MR.
PATTERSON'S
TOY BOX

As Jana and her friend Rita walked to Jana's house after school one day, they passed the house next door. With the garage door up, they could see into Mr. Patterson's workshop.

"Ol' Stingy is working away in there," Jana said, referring to Mr. Patterson. "He never wants to share."

"Why do you call him that?" Rita asked. "Isn't he the one who gives you a birthday card every year? And don't forget Christmas. He always brings you peanut brittle," she reminded her friend.

"I know, but he has that big box of toys in his garage," argued Jana, "and he's so stingy, he won't even give me one."

"Well, he must have a good reason," said Rita.

Jana remembered the day she first saw the boxful of wooden toys. Mr. Patterson was cleaning the shelves in his garage when Jana wandered in. "Where did you get these?" she asked, pointing to the toys.

"Leave those alone!" he snapped. He never did answer her question. So Jana stomped home and called him Stingy ever since.

Then one day, Jana peeked into Mr. Patterson's cluttered workshop and saw him digging through a boxful of scrap wood. "Whatcha doin'?" she called.

"Oh, nothing much," replied Mr. Patterson. "I'm just deciding what piece would make the best elephant."

"Elephant?" Jana laughed.

"Elephant," Mr. Patterson answered curtly. "For the children's home."

Jana's eyes brightened. "You mean you make toys all by yourself?" she asked in disbelief.

"That's what I mean," said Mr. Patterson, returning to his work. "I whittle."

Jana's face felt hot as she recalled the times she'd talked about Mr. Patterson behind his back—like what she had said to Rita. She stepped up to his workbench and cleared her throat. "Mr. Patterson?" she began. Her stomach did flip-flops. "I . . . uh . . . think you're very generous to whittle for the children."

A wide toothy smile filled Mr. Patterson's wrinkled face. "And I think you're very generous to notice," he said.

> An anxious heart weighs a
> man down, but a kind word
> cheers him up.
>
> Proverbs 12:25

Kwitcherbellyakin

▶▶▶▶▶▶▶▶▶▶▶▶▶

Something to Remember

God wants me to speak kindly
about everyone.

Questions for Family Discussion

1. What was Jana's big mistake?
2. Have you ever unkindly labeled someone just because you didn't understand that person?
3. Do you think God understands what you're really like?

Write a Family Prayer

_____

_____

_____

_____

30

>>>>>>>>>>>>>>>>>>>>>>>>>>>>>>>>>>>

THE BEST ANSWER

Kayla and her cousin, Trish, are the same age. They are a lot alike. They both like to read, they both love chocolate pudding, and they both gag at the very mention of scrambled eggs.

But whenever they spend a weekend together, Kayla and Trish always end up arguing. If Kayla wins at a game of checkers, for instance, Trish claims that she must have cheated. If Trish says she got an *A* in math, Kayla gets jealous and says, "Well, my teacher gave me an *A +* for extra effort."

One morning Kayla's mom had heard enough. "Somebody had better come up with a solution to this ridiculous arguing, or I'm going to have to drive Trish home."

Kayla glared across the room at Trish. "You're trying to ruin my weekend!"

Trish scowled back. "You always start everything!"

"Here," said Mother, interrupting their little

feud. "You can fold these towels while you decide how you're going to get along."

Kayla folded a fluffy pink towel lengthwise.

"You're doing it the wrong way," argued Trish, folding hers differently.

Kayla felt like screaming but decided to try something sneaky instead.

Every time Trish criticized her, Kayla just tried to think of something else. She even pretended she was folding towels for the Queen of England.

Finally, Trish could stand the silence no longer. "What's wrong with you, anyway?" she said, eyeing her cousin suspiciously. "You're being too nice all of a sudden. How come you're so quiet?"

Kayla stacked her pile of neatly folded towels in Mom's laundry basket. "Sometimes the best answer is no answer at all," she said.

> **Let us therefore make every effort to do what leads to peace.**
>
> Romans 14:19

▸▸▸▸▸▸▸▸▸▸▸▸▸▸

Something to Remember

God helps me avoid arguments.

Questions for Family Discussion

1. Do you know anyone who seems to enjoy arguing?

2. What are some good ways to avoid a disagreement?
3. Do you ever argue with God?

Write a Family Prayer

_____

_____

_____

Kwitcherbellyakin

31

THE BIG MOVE

One day Andrew's father treated him to lunch at their favorite pizza place. While they ate and talked, Dad broke some unbelievable news. "Son, the company is transferring me in June. We'll be moving to Colorado."

Andrew's throat tightened. "But Dad," he argued, "I thought we'd never, ever leave Glenmore. This is our home." The picture of saying good-bye to friends and relatives flashed through Andrew's mind like a sad movie.

"And what about school?" he quickly added. "I won't know anybody there."

Dad laid his hand on top of Andrew's and looked into his son's eyes. "I know," he said gently. "I wish we had a choice but we don't. I wanted to tell you today, though, so you'd have plenty of time to get used to the idea." Dad paused. "God will provide exactly what each of us needs, including new friends," he told him. "You'll see."

Andrew pushed his half-eaten slice of pizza away. "What if I don't want new friends?" he protested. He got up quickly, ran out to the car, and slammed the door.

Dad drove home in silence.

Then, just as they rounded the corner at the end of their street, Andrew grabbed the dashboard. "Watch out, Dad!" he cried. "There's a turtle in the road."

Sure enough, a small, determined box turtle was inching its way across the intersection.

Dad pulled to the curb and stopped the car. "I wonder where he's going?"

"What if he's lost? Maybe we ought to take him home," suggested Andrew.

"But if we take him to our house, he might be confused," said Dad, "and very homesick."

Andrew cast Dad a knowing glance. "Come on, Dad." He laughed. "A turtle can be happy anywhere if it has the right shelter and food."

Dad reached over and patted Andrew's shoulder. "You're absolutely right," he said gently. "He'll feel right at home in no time at all."

> **My God will meet all your needs according to his glorious riches in Christ Jesus.**
>
> Philippians 4:19

▶▶▶▶▶▶▶▶▶▶▶▶▶

Something to Remember

God will always give me what I need.

Questions for Family Discussion

1. Have you ever had a friend who moved away?
2. How might you help someone who has to move?
3. What are some good ways to welcome a new arrival in town?
4. How does God help us through times of change?

Write a Family Prayer

_____

_____

_____

_____

32

▸▸▸▸▸▸▸▸▸▸▸▸▸▸▸▸▸▸▸▸▸▸▸▸▸▸▸▸▸

THE NIGHT
THE LIGHTS
WENT OUT

Vince and Gene were watching a spooky movie on TV. Outside, wild storm winds tugged at the window screens, adding to the eerie atmosphere.

Then, without warning, all the lights in the house flickered out. "Mom! Dad!" called Vince. "The electricity's out."

There was no answer.

"Maybe they went next door to visit Mr. and Mrs. Tran," said Gene. "Mr. Tran came home from the hospital yesterday."

"Maybe," Vince answered quietly.

"Do you have a flashlight?" asked Gene. His voice sounded high and shaky.

"I think there's one in the kitchen drawer," said Vince. "We'll just have to feel our way along the walls."

Gene followed his friend across the living room at a snail's pace. Whenever a bolt of lightning flashed, the two would jump. Even their shadows on the walls startled them.

"Ouch!" Vince yelled. "I bumped into a dining room chair." He stopped and rubbed his toe a minute. "I'd sure hate to be blind."

"Yeah, me too," joked Gene, "especially if you were my guide."

A sudden flash of lightning zigzagged across the dark sky. Gene and Vince caught sight of each other and screamed. Then they fell to the floor in laughter.

"Forget the flashlight," Vince finally decided.

"OK. Let's just sit here and watch the lightning," suggested Gene.

So the two friends knelt by the dining room window and admired God's awesome light show.

"Hey, this is better than fireworks on the Fourth of July," said Vince.

"Yeah," agreed Gene, "and we've got a great view!"

> **The heavens declare the glory of God; the skies proclaim the work of his hands.**
>
> Psalm 19:1

▸▸▸▸▸▸▸▸▸▸▸▸▸▸

Something to Remember

God lights my darkest night with His power and love.

Questions for Family Discussion

1. Has the electricity ever gone off at your house during a storm?
2. What do you think about when you stare up into the night sky?
3. Is there anything to fear about the darkness?
4. How do you think God's love can light the darkness?

Write a Family Prayer

_____

_____

_____

_____

Kwitcherbellyakin

33

>>>>>>>>>>>>>>>>>>>>>>>>>>>>>>>>>>>

RICKY'S SPECIAL PROJECT

Ricky wanted to surprise his sister, Leah, with a special gift, so he called her into his room one day. "Lie down on this big piece of paper," he told her. "I'm going to draw around you with a pencil."

Three-year-old Leah lay still as a statue while Ricky traced around her curly hair and all the way down to her toes. She didn't even move when the pencil tickled her neck.

"Am I through?" asked Leah, not daring to blink.

"Yes. You can get up now," Ricky told her. "But go somewhere to play. I need to be alone for a few minutes to finish the surprise."

Leah visited her dolls, who were all suffering from a virus. She told them about Ricky's project. "He had to make lines all the way around me," she said.

While Leah cared for her sick dolls, Ricky busily cut out his life-sized Leah poster. Next he

drew curly brown hair, big brown eyes, a tiny nose, and a lopsided grin.

"Ricky," yelled Leah, "are you finished yet?"

"No, not yet!" he called back, guarding his surprise.

He colored a blue blouse and pink pants on the Leah poster. He even drew fuzzy socks and sneakers with pink flowers all over them—just like the ones Leah was wearing.

"Can't I see it yet?" begged Leah, breathing through the keyhole.

"In a minute," said Ricky. He found some buttons among the craft supplies his mother kept for them and glued the buttons on the shirt. Then he added some shoestrings for the sneakers.

Finally Ricky walked over to the door and whispered through the keyhole. "Leah," he said, "you can come and see your surprise now."

Kwitcherbellyakin

Leah burst into the room. Her mouth flew wide open when she saw the life-sized Leah doll lying on Ricky's bed.

"It's me! It's me!" she cried. "And you made it all by yourself."

Ricky felt good about his surprise. And he felt even better when his little sister planted a big, sloppy kiss on his cheek.

> **He has made everything beautiful in its time.**
>
> Ecclesiastes 3:11

▶▶▶▶▶▶▶▶▶▶▶▶▶

Something to Remember

God takes His time to do everything right.

Questions for Family Discussion

1. Why did Ricky want to surprise his sister?
2. What would life be like if God had made us all the same?
3. How is each person in your family unique?

Write a Family Prayer

_____

_____

_____

_____

34

>>>

THE RUNAWAY DOG

At a neighborhood barbecue, Shannon's friend Wanda decided to walk her dog.

"Do you want to come?" Wanda asked.

"I don't know if I should," Shannon replied.

"If you come with me, I'll let you hold Elmer's leash on the way back," Wanda promised.

"I need to tell Daddy where we're going," Shannon said.

"He's busy talking to my dad," said Wanda, pointing to a group of men gathered around the barbecue grill. "Let's just walk Elmer and come back real quick."

"OK," agreed Shannon. "But remember, I get a turn holding his leash."

Wanda let Elmer lead the way, and he dragged them across an overgrown lot next to her house. The weeds scratched their legs and made them itch.

Shannon, who had allergies every spring, began to sneeze over and over again. "Something funny must be growing here," she said between sneezes.

"C'mon, Elmer," scolded Wanda. "Let's go this way. Shannon and I don't like this field."

Shannon turned to see how far they had come. She gasped. "We shouldn't be this far away from the barbecue," she said. "I can hardly see my house."

"It's OK." Wanda laughed. "I come here all the time with Elmer. He knows the way back."

"But I'm supposed to ask my dad before I go this far," argued Shannon.

Wanda wasn't a bit worried. "We can circle around by those trees over there and be back at the barbecue before I count to a hundred."

But Elmer had other plans. In one quick jerk, he yanked himself free and loped happily through the tall weeds.

"Elmer!" called Wanda. "Come back!"

Elmer ignored Wanda and kept running.

"C'mon," said Wanda, pulling Shannon across the field. "We've got to catch him."

"OK," Shannon said, but inside she wished she had never left the barbecue. *What will I tell Daddy?* she thought.

> **"In your unfailing love you will lead the people you have redeemed."**
>
> Exodus 15:13

▶▶▶▶▶▶▶▶▶▶▶▶

Something to Remember
God leads me in the right paths.

THE RUNAWAY DOG

Questions for Family Discussion

1. Have you ever gotten into trouble playing follow the leader?
2. What should you do if a friend encourages you to disobey God or your parents? Is that person a true friend?
3. Will Jesus ever lead us into trouble?

Write a Family Prayer

_____

_____

_____

_____

35

➤➤➤➤➤➤➤➤➤➤➤➤➤➤➤➤➤➤➤➤➤➤➤➤➤➤➤➤➤➤➤➤

THE WORRY BOX

Angie worried about everything. She worried about tests at school. She worried about whether rain would spoil their picnic. She worried about who would care for her if something happened to her parents.

Angie worried so much that her grandmother called her a worrywart.

"What's a worrywart?" asked Angie.

Grandma closed her eyes, searching for an answer. "Well," she said, "a worrywart is a person like you who always looks for something to worry about."

"But I don't like that name," protested Angie. "It sounds weird."

"That's because worrying *is* weird," said Grandma.

Grandma took Angie's hand and led her outside.

"See that tree?" she asked, pointing to a full, leafy elm. "Remember how worried you were when that robin's nest tumbled to the ground last spring?"

"Yes," Angie replied, "but that's because I thought the babies would be hurt."

"And what about your little black kitten?" asked Grandma. "Remember the night you hardly slept?"

Angie nodded. "I was worried because I thought the kitten had run away and wouldn't come back."

Grandma lovingly smoothed Angie's long, silky hair. "I know," she said. "You were worried because you loved the kitten and didn't know if it would be able to care for itself."

Angie thought back to that dark, sleepless night. "But then I asked God to bring her home," she reminded Grandma. "And He did, remember?"

Grandma and Angie walked back into the house. "Look at this," said Grandma, taking a blue tin from the window sill. "Do you know what this is?"

Angie shook her head.

"It's my worry box." explained Grandma. "Whenever I start to fret, I write down my worry on a slip of paper and drop it in the box. Then I pray and ask God to take care of each worry."

"Does it work?" asked Angie.

"Every time," said Grandma. "And the best part is that *I'm* not a worrywart anymore."

> You will keep in perfect peace
> him whose mind is steadfast,
> because he trusts in you.
>
> Isaiah 26:3

▶▶▶▶▶▶▶▶▶▶▶▶▶

Something to Remember
God helps me not to worry.

Questions for Family Discussion
1. Is there ever a good reason to worry?
2. How can worrying hurt us?
3. Do you think God ever worries?

Write a Family Prayer

_____

_____

_____

_____

36

>>>>>>>>>>>>>>>>>>>>>>>>>>>>>>>>>>>

THE SUMMER FRIEND

Ted met a summer friend one July when his family vacationed at a cabin in the mountains. He and Dad were unpacking the car when he heard someone say, "Can I help?"

Ted turned around to see a boy about his age with hair almost the color of carrots.

"Sure, why not?" said Dad. "Here, you can carry one of these bags."

"My name's Jon," said the boy, "but my parents still call me Jonathan."

"Don't feel bad." Ted laughed. "My mom calls me Theodore most of the time, but I'd rather be called Ted."

Ted and Jon spent long afternoons fishing in the creek that bubbled behind Ted's cabin. At night they told stories around a small campfire that Dad built for them in the meadow. One night they even got to pitch a tent and sleep outside.

But when it came time to say good-bye, Ted swallowed a sad lump in this throat. "I had fun," he said, digging his toe in the soft grass.

"Me, too," Jon answered quietly. He fidgeted inside his pocket and handed Ted a folded piece of paper. "Here's my address," he said, biting his lip. "Want to write?"

"Sure," said Ted. "And maybe next summer we can both come here again."

Ted and Jon wrote every week for the rest of the summer. Ted kept all of his friend's letters in a box under his bed.

When school started in the fall, though, the letters from Jon stopped coming. Ted still wrote every week, hoping to get an answer.

"Any mail today?" he would ask after school, but the answer was always the same—no.

Ted dropped one last letter into the mailbox. "I thought we'd be friends forever, no matter what," he wrote to Jon, "but maybe I was wrong."

He talked to Dad about it. "I don't understand," he told him. "We planned to meet at the cabin next summer and everything."

Dad gave Ted an understanding hug. "I know it's disappointing, son," he said, "but sometimes even the best of friends get too busy for each other."

"I the Lord do not change."

Malachi 3:6

▸▸▸▸▸▸▸▸▸▸▸▸▸

Something to Remember

God is a friend who will never change.

THE SUMMER FRIEND   **117**

Questions for Family Discussion

1. Have you ever had a summer friend?
2. Why does a friendship sometimes fade away?
3. How does God prove His faithfulness?

Write a Family Prayer

Kwitcherbellyakin

37

>>

LIMPY

Doreen was born with a serious bone disease. When she was younger, she had to stay at the children's hospital several times, and a skilled surgeon built special hip and knee joints for her. "Without the surgery," he had explained to her parents, "she won't be able to walk."

Doreen hardly ever complained. In fact, neighbors and friends who visited her in the hospital came away wearing smiles instead of worried frowns.

"Soon I'll be able to run faster than any of you," she often joked.

Doreen was excited when the surgeries were all over. Now she would be able to climb the jungle gym with the other kids. She could finally crawl through the long, winding tubes at the park and sit in a chair without hurting anymore. Only one problem remained: Doreen had a limp.

She had almost gotten used to the pain that shot down her legs. But hard as she tried, she couldn't get used to the deep pain in her heart every time she heard the taunting as she limped by.

"Hey, there's Limpy," some of her classmates would chant.

"Just ignore them, Doreen," her friends advised her. "They're just ignorant, that's all."

One morning Mr. Adams, the friendly school custodian, pulled Doreen aside in the hallway. "Know why they're teasin' you, Doreen?" he asked.

"No," she replied, "but I'd like to trade places with them for just one hour to shut them up."

Mr. Adams lifted her chin and looked into her eyes. "They're jealous of your *secret*," he whispered.

Kwitcherbellyakin

Doreen looked confused. "What secret?" she asked. "I don't have a secret."

"Sure you do." Mr. Adams chuckled. "You know the secret to being happy inside, and no one can take that away from you."

> **Whatever happens, conduct yourself in a manner worthy of the gospel of Christ.**
>
> Philippians 1:27

▶▶▶▶▶▶▶▶▶▶▶▶▶

Something to Remember

God gives me a joyful heart even when I'm not feeling happy on the outside.

Questions for Family Discussion

1. What would cause someone to ridicule a handicapped person?
2. How do you make yourself feel better when you're having a rough day?
3. Does it matter how we react when we hear unkind remarks?

Write a Family Prayer

_____

_____

_____

_____

LIMPY

38

>>>>>>>>>>>>>>>>>>>>>>>>>>>>>>>>>>>>

DREADING THANKSGIVING

Thanksgiving was always a special event for Valerie's family. Aunts, uncles, and cousins came from miles away to meet at Grandma and Grandpa's house. Valerie usually looked forward to seeing all of her relatives—but not this year.

"Mom," she moaned. "I feel sort of *blah,* like somebody pulled a plug and let all my energy out."

Mom laid a cool hand across Valerie's forehead, the way concerned mothers usually do.

"Hmmm," she said, "you feel cool as a cucumber and look like you're healthy as a horse."

"Oh, Mom," mumbled Valerie. "I don't feel like a cucumber or a horse. I just feel *blah.*"

"Describe it," suggested Mom.

Valerie rolled her eyes. "I feel all keyed up and tired at the same time. I think I need to stay home tomorrow."

"On Thanksgiving?" screeched Mom. "Sorry, Val. It's a big day, and unless you have a fever or sore throat, there's no reason to miss it."

Valerie crossed her arms stubbornly. "If I was 'beautiful baby Kristin,' I would get to stay home if I even burped wrong."

"So that's it, huh?" answered Mom. "You're jealous of your new baby cousin?"

"Jealous?" mimicked Valerie. "Of a fat little baby who gets tons of presents from everybody? Ha!"

Mom smoothed Valerie's bedspread and sat next to her. "You know, Val, there was a Thanksgiving many years ago when *you* were the fat little baby who got all the attention."

Valerie was too embarrassed to look at her mother.

"Grandma and Grandpa have plenty of love to go around," Mom continued, "and there's no danger of it running out."

"Well . . ." Valerie laughed. "Maybe I'll feel cool as a cucumber and healthy as a horse by morning."

"Or maybe you'll just feel like yourself again," said Mom.

> **Search me, O God, and know my heart; test me and know my anxious thoughts.**
>
> Psalm 139:23

▶▶▶▶▶▶▶▶▶▶▶▶

Something to Remember

God understands my deepest feelings even when I don't.

DREADING THANKSGIVING

Questions for Family Discussion

1. What do the words *heart* and *anxious thoughts* in today's verse have to do with being jealous?
2. What lesson did Valerie learn by talking it over with her mom?
3. What would you say to someone who was acting jealous?

Write a Family Prayer

_____

_____

_____

_____

Kwitcherbellyakin

39

>>

THE TROUBLESOME CONTEST

Bill arrived on the first day of vacation Bible school to discover a huge banner hanging across the front of the church. *Bring-a-Friend Contest,* it read. *Sign up here!*

"What's the contest for?" he asked Pastor Ray.

"It's a special challenge," said Pastor Ray. "Whoever brings the most friends this week wins a brand-new Bible."

A new Bible! Bill always borrowed his dad's heavy brown Bible then returned it to him after church each Sunday. "I have lots of friends," he boasted. "Winning the Bible will be easy."

Pastor Ray patted him on the back. "Well, then, I guess you have lots of telephoning to do," he said with a grin.

That afternoon, Bill phoned everyone he could think of. "Would you like to come to vacation Bible school tomorrow?" he asked.

"Thanks," said Ronnie, "but no, thanks. I'm going to a ball game with my uncle and aunt."

"I can't," explained Phil. "I'm going to the coast for three days."

"Are you kidding?" Manuel laughed. "I went last year, and I didn't like it, remember?"

Even Sam, who would usually go anywhere with Bill, had plans. "Sorry, I have a dentist's appointment," he explained.

Bill's heart sank. *So much for the new Bible,* he thought.

The next morning when Bill arrived at Bible school, Pastor Ray came up to him with a big smile on his face. "So, how did your telephone campaign go?" he asked.

Bill hung his head. "Terrible," he admitted. "I phoned everybody, but nobody could come. I feel all twisted inside, like a pretzel."

Pastor Ray understood Bill's disappointment. "Winning a new Bible was important to you, Bill," he said, "but there's something even more important than that."

"What could be more important than a brand-new Bible?" wondered Bill.

"Your love for God," said Pastor Ray. "That's something that you can share with your friends anywhere, even if they won't come to vacation Bible school."

Never be lacking in zeal, but keep your spiritual fervor, serving the Lord.

Romans 12:11

Kwitcherbellyakin

▶▶▶▶▶▶▶▶▶▶▶▶▶

Something to Remember

God gives me challenges to help me grow.

Questions for Family Discussion

1. Do you like contests?
2. Can we force someone to love God?
3. Has God given you a special challenge lately? What have you done about it?

Write a Family Prayer

_____

_____

_____

_____

40

>>

ACCIDENT IN
THE WOOD SHOP

Kenton wandered into his dad's wood shop one Saturday and found Dad working on a pair of heart-shaped bookends.

"Would you like to help?" Dad asked.

Kenton ran his hand over the wood pieces that Dad had sanded smooth. "Could I make something of my very own?" he asked. "Like maybe a box to keep my race cars in?" His gray eyes begged Dad for a yes.

Dad searched through a pile of wood scraps. "Sure," he said, handing Kenton a few pieces, "but be very careful."

Kenton pulled a stool up to the workbench and got to work. First he drew a straight line across a ten-inch piece of wood. "Need a little help with that saw?" Dad offered.

"No, I've done this before," said Kenton.

He held the saw carefully, the way Dad had taught him. But before it had a chance to even scratch the wood, the jagged-edged blade slipped.

A dull, throbbing sensation filled Kenton's left index finger.

"Dad, I'm bleeding!"

Dad hurried over to his son. "That looks deep," he said. He grabbed a clean rag. "Here." He handed Kenton the thick white cloth. "Wrap this around your finger and squeeze hard. It'll slow the bleeding until we can get you to Dr. Bayne's."

Fortunately, the doctor's office was only a few blocks away, and minutes later Kenton was sitting on a white-covered table in an examining room.

Dr. Bayne had a special way of calming kids. "Been working in that workshop again, eh, Kenton?" he said calmly, inspecting the cut.

Kenton managed a grin. "Yeah, I just started making a box for my race cars," he told the doctor. "I was in a hurry, I guess."

Dr. Bayne chatted with Kenton and his Dad as he cleaned, stitched, and bandaged the cut.

"How long will it take to heal?" Kenton asked.

Dr. Bayne scratched his head. "Well," he said, raising his silvery eyebrows, "God usually mends a finger in about ten to fourteen days."

On the short drive home, Kenton looked down at his bandaged finger. "It doesn't hurt as much now."

"That's the way God works," said Dad. "It will still take some time, but God heals our cuts and bruises on the outside and even our hurt feelings on the inside."

What a great God! thought Kenton.

ACCIDENT IN THE WOOD SHOP

O Lord my God, I called to
you for help and you healed
me.

Psalm 30:2

▶▶▶▶▶▶▶▶▶▶▶▶▶▶▶

Something to Remember

God heals every kind of hurt and
makes me well again.

Questions for Family Discussion

1. Have you ever had to get stitches?
2. Can you think of a time when you accidentally hurt someone else's feelings?
3. Have you ever gotten your feelings hurt?
4. How can we get over any kind of hurt?

Write a Family Prayer

_____

_____

_____

_____

41

▶▶▶▶▶▶▶▶▶▶▶▶▶▶▶▶▶▶▶▶▶▶▶▶▶▶▶

EMILY'S PITY PARTY

One day Emily held a pity party for herself. "Nobody likes me!" she sobbed into her pillow. "They think I'm either too young, too stupid, or too short!"

Just then her mother knocked on the bedroom door. "Care if I come in?" Mom asked.

Tears dribbled like miniature rivers down Emily's cheeks. "Sure, come on in," she called, trying to sound cheerful.

"Grandma just called," said Mom. "She's feeling a little better today."

Emily managed a smile. "Good," she said. "Does that mean we can visit her?"

"As a matter of fact, yes," said Mom, "and that's why Grandma called. She wondered if you would like to come over and take a walk with her in a few minutes."

"I don't know. . . ." said Emily.

"It would really help Grandma to have a walking partner," Mom explained. "She's still a little shaky from the surgery."

"Well, all right," Emily said, reaching for her blue sweater. "I'll go."

Emily hurried the two and a half blocks to Grandma's house and then strolled with her Grandma down to the street corner and back. That was all her grandmother could manage. They both talked some, but mostly Emily listened while her grandma described the "good old days."

When they returned to Grandma's cozy little house, Emily helped fix them each a tuna sandwich.

"I hated to interrupt your day," said her grandmother, "but I'm so glad you came. I feel better just having you here to talk to!"

"Thanks, Grandma." Emily kissed her grandmother's cheek. "You couldn't have interrupted me at a better time."

> The LORD upholds all those
> who fall and lifts up all who
> are bowed down.
>
> Psalm 145:14

▶▶▶▶▶▶▶▶▶▶▶▶▶

Something to Remember

God takes my mind off my problems
when I help others.

Questions for Family Discussion

1. Have you had a pity party for yourself lately?
2. How do you think God feels about pity parties?

Kwitcherbellyakin

3. What happens when we start thinking of others?
4. Why did Grandma feel better having Emily with her?

Write a Family Prayer

_____

_____

_____

_____

42

>>

ANYBODY HOME?

One day while Natalie was skipping home from the park for lunch, she stopped to admire a tiny green frog lying in the sun. Then she spotted a line of busy ants carrying a large bread crumb. After following them awhile, she looked up and saw a cute little poodle chasing a squirrel across the street.

When Natalie turned at the next corner, she thought of the hot lunch that would be waiting for her. "Chicken noodle soup—my favorite," she said to herself.

Something was wrong, though. Where was the lilac bush that hugged her bedroom window? What happened to the fern that usually hung by the front door?

I'm lost! Natalie suddenly realized. *This isn't my street at all!* Tears stung her eyes as she tried to decide which way to turn.

Natalie peered up and down the street. At the end of the block stood a building that she saw every day from her school bus window. "There's

God's house," she said aloud. She ran toward the church as fast as she could go.

Huffing and puffing, Natalie flung open the heavy door of the church and called out, "Is anybody home?"

A man with a friendly smile poked his head out of an office door down the hallway. "Hello," he said. "How may I help you, young lady?"

"I was walking home, but I think I followed too many frogs and ants and dogs. I might be lost or something."

"Well, I'm Pastor Washington," said the man, "and you've come to the right place for help. Would you like to use my phone?"

Natalie repeated her phone number in her head and dialed carefully. "Four-two-six, seven-five-nine-one."

When Daddy arrived, Natalie introduced him to Pastor Washington. "Pastor Washington said that it's a good thing I came to God's house," she said.

"It's the *best* place to come when you're lost or feel alone," agreed Daddy.

"Or anytime at all," added Pastor Washington.

> I rejoiced with those who said
> to me, "Let us go to the house
> of the Lord."
>
> Psalm 122:1

ANYBODY HOME?   **135**

▶▶▶▶▶▶▶▶▶▶▶▶▶▶

Something to Remember

God's house is a place to find
help and comfort.

Questions for Family Discussion

1. Have you ever gotten lost on the way home? How did it make you feel?
2. Have you memorized your address and phone number?
3. What is so special about God's house?
4. Can a person ever be lost from God?

Write a Family Prayer

_____

_____

_____

_____

Kwitcherbellyakin

43
>>>

A SILLY NAME

Brian's parents nicknamed him Hot Dog when he was four years old. Why? Because every time Mama asked, "What would you like to eat, Brian?" he'd answer, "Twenty hundred hot dogs!"

But his nickname was a family secret. No one but Brian, Mama, Daddy, and his two brothers knew about it. They never called him Hot Dog in front of his friends at the ball park. They never called him anything but Brian at church. And they never, ever called him Hot Dog when they had visitors.

Except once—when his mother slipped.

Brian was playing in the family room with some friends when Mama came home from the grocery store. Just as she was carrying two heavy sacks of groceries into the kitchen, the phone rang.

"Hot Dog!" she hollered. "Would you please answer the phone?"

Brian wanted to disappear like a snowflake on a warm windowpane. His friends stared at him, their mouths flung open wide.

"*Hot Dog*?" they squealed. Then raising their voices to a high pitch, they copied Mama. "Hot Dog, would you please answer the phone?" Then they rolled on the floor, laughing.

Brian raced for the telephone, happy to escape his friends' teasing.

Later, he made his friends promise to keep his nickname a secret. "Only one other Person besides my family knows my nickname," said Brian, "and He's very trustworthy."

"Who's that?" his friends wanted to know.

Kwitcherbellyakin

"God," said Brian.

Brian's friends just shook their heads and laughed.

"Hey, don't laugh," said Brian. "God even calls me Hot Dog sometimes, but only when we're alone."

"I am the good shepherd; I know my sheep and my sheep know me."

John 10:14

▶▶▶▶▶▶▶▶▶▶▶▶▶▶

Something to Remember

God knows everything about me— and He loves me!

Questions for Family Discussion

1. Has your family given you a secret nickname?
2. Do you know God as well as He knows you?
3. How can you get to know Him better?
4. Are all your secrets safe with God?

Write a Family Prayer

_____

_____

_____

_____

44

>>>>>>>>>>>>>>>>>>>>>>>>>>>>>>>>>>>

CANCEL ALL FLIGHTS

One Christmas, Carrie and her parents planned a trip to Uncle Vito's house. Uncle Vito lived far, far away in Missouri.

Carrie sat in the airport with her parents, waiting to board the plane. Hugging her doll sleepily, Carrie whispered to her mother, "When will our seats be ready?"

Mommy squeezed her hand. "The plane's a little slow today, honey. The pilot has to be extra careful because of the snow."

Carrie repeated Mommy's words to her doll, Winifred. Then she looked up at her mother. "I told Winifred to sit still and be patient," she said. "She's starting to get grouchy."

Carrie was about to doze off when an announcement cut through the noisy airport. "All flights have been cancelled. Please report to your ticket agent for more information."

Daddy looked at Mommy and sighed. Mommy glanced at Carrie and sighed. And Carrie whispered to her doll, "Better be *real* patient now, Winifred."

Carrie followed her parents to the ticket booth, and her daddy spoke to a lady in a blue uniform. "What's the problem, ma'am?" he asked.

"Severe weather makes flying impossible this evening, sir," explained the lady. She showed Daddy a long list with names and numbers on it. "There's another flight leaving first thing in the morning if the weather improves."

CANCEL ALL FLIGHTS

Daddy thanked her and leaned down to talk to Carrie. "Tell Winifred that we can't always count on the weather," he said, "but we *can* count on the One who controls the weather."

> Give thanks to the LORD, for he is good; his love endures forever.
>
> 1 Chronicles 16:34

▶▶▶▶▶▶▶▶▶▶▶▶

Something to Remember

God won't ever cancel His love for me.

Questions for Family Discussion

1. Have you ever taken a trip by plane?
2. How do you feel when your plans are delayed?
3. How does God help us when we're disappointed?
4. Does God ever change like the weather?

Write a Family Prayer

_____

_____

_____

_____

45

▸▸▸▸▸▸▸▸▸▸▸▸▸▸▸▸▸▸▸▸▸▸▸▸▸▸▸▸▸▸▸

JUST A PEEK

One day, Elizabeth was standing in a line at her Aunt Marian's donut shop. Aunt Marian had set a giant jar of jelly beans on the glass counter with a hand-lettered sign on it. The sign read: Guess How Many Beans Are in the Jar and Win a Bike.

Elizabeth leaned against the counter and studied the jar. "There must be at least a million jelly beans in there," she told Aunt Marian.

"Maybe, maybe not," Aunt Marian replied. She ran a dust rag over the jar and grinned.

"Only Aunt Marian knows the answer," she teased. "I've got it written on a slip of paper right here," she said, patting her apron pocket. "It's Top Secret information, for sure."

Elizabeth didn't care about a new bike for herself because she received one for her birthday. But her friend Kim was stuck with an old dilapidated hand-me-down bike from an older brother.

Think how excited Kim would be if she won a new bike, thought Elizabeth. *Maybe I'll peek in Aunt Marian's apron pocket after work when she hangs it on the hook by the door. What's the harm if it helps Kim?*

But later that day, just as she was about to sneak a look, something inside her bothered her. She couldn't do it.

Elizabeth left the store with the image of the jar in her mind. "Let's see if I can't figure it out by myself," she said.

> **Because he himself suffered when he was tempted, he is able to help those who are being tempted.**
>
> Hebrews 2:18

▸▸▸▸▸▸▸▸▸▸▸▸▸▸▸

Something to Remember

God helps me to be honest.

Questions for Family Discussion

1. Is there ever a good reason to cheat?
2. How would you feel if someone won something for you dishonestly?
3. What would you say if you caught a friend cheating?

Write a Family Prayer

_____

_____

_____

46

>>>>>>>>>>>>>>>>>>>>>>>>>>>>>>>>>>

IF ONLY I COULD BE ...

In Sunday school one morning before class started, Patty was complaining about the way she looked. "I wish my eyes were sky blue instead of brown," she said. "And I'd give anything to have honey-blond hair clear down to here." She pointed to her waist.

"Not me," said Tara. "I hate my frizzy blond hair. I'd rather have shiny dark hair and green eyes, like a cat."

Mrs. Peters, their Sunday school teacher, laughed. "Well, I guess we all have things we'd like to change," she said. "I'd like to be thinner, but losing weight is hard work."

Mrs. Peters studied the faces seated around the table. "Each of you looks the way you look because God took His time creating you. Patty, your brown eyes are no mistake. Neither is Tara's blond hair."

Patty frowned. "But Mrs. Peters, what if we don't like the way we look? What should we do?"

"Well," Mrs. Peters replied, "you can start by

IF ONLY I COULD BE ...

thinking of all that you *have* and thanking God for that."

"Like good health and my family—stuff like that?" asked Tara.

"Exactly," said Mrs. Peters. "Then you can look around you and see how you might help others who aren't as fortunate."

"But what does that have to do with wanting a different hair color?" asked Tara.

"When we take our eyes off ourselves and think of others, what we look like doesn't seem as important," Mrs. Peters said. "And we often realize just how blessed we are."

Suddenly Patty giggled. "I guess I'm blessed to have any hair at all," she said with a silly grin, "'cause my parents said that I was born *bald!*"

> For you created my inmost
> being; you knit me together in
> my mother's womb.
>
> Psalm 139:13

▶▶▶▶▶▶▶▶▶▶▶▶▶

Something to Remember

God made me the way He wanted me to
be, and He loves the way I look.

Questions for Family Discussion

1. Do you like the way you look?
2. How do you feel, knowing that God saw your very first moment of life?

3. How do you think God feels when we complain about how He made us?
4. Have you ever thanked God for making you unique?

Write a Family Prayer

_____

_____

_____

_____

47

THE TWO-LETTER WORD

Eddie wanted to play over at his friend Doug's house after school on Thursday. "All the guys will be there after school today," he told his mother. "We're going to watch TV and play in his tree house and . . . "

"Hold on one minute, Edward," said Mom. "Has Doug cleared this with his mother?"

"Uh . . . I think so," answered Eddie.

"And what, exactly, did she say?" continued Mom.

"She says it's all right," mumbled Eddie.

Mom seemed to notice that nervous little twitch forming in the corner of Eddie's mouth. "Well, then, let me give her a call and see what time I should pick you up."

Eddie's eyes widened. "But she doesn't get home from work until six o'clock," he blurted. "How about if you just pick me up around four-thirty?"

Mom folded her arms and looked directly into

his eyes. "Eddie," she said, "what have I told you about playing at Doug's house?"

Eddie toyed with a loose button on his shirt. "You said that I can't go there unless an adult is home."

Mom waited for Eddie to continue.

"Please say yes this time," he begged.

Mom shook her head. "I'm sorry," she said. "Maybe another time. My answer is no. N-O."

"I'll be half grown by the time I get to play with my friends," grumbled Eddie.

Later that evening, Mom sat at the kitchen table and made a few phone calls. When she got off the phone, she told Eddie, "Don't be late coming home from school tomorrow. A few of your friends will be coming over to *our* house."

"All right, Mom!" Eddie yelled, punching the air.

Mom had a twinkle in her eye. "I warned them to hurry, though, because you were almost half grown and they might not recognize you," she kidded.

> **Children, obey your parents in everything, for this pleases the Lord.**
>
> Colossians 3:20

▶▶▶▶▶▶▶▶▶▶▶▶▶

Something to Remember

God helps me accept my parents' decisions.

Questions for Family Discussion

1. Have you ever expected a yes but received a no?
2. Why is obeying your parents so important?
3. When we are obedient to our parents, whom else are we obeying?

Write a Family Prayer

_____

_____

_____

_____

48

▶▶▶▶▶▶▶▶▶▶▶▶▶▶▶▶▶▶▶▶▶▶▶▶▶▶▶▶▶▶

SENG'S PRECIOUS LAMB

Seng received a beautiful ceramic lamb from her aunt who lived in Thailand. Seng set the lamb on her dresser alongside a new mirror and brush set.

"Don't you dare touch my lamb," she warned her brothers. "It's very fragile."

Then one Saturday, while Seng was sweeping the hardwood floor in her room, she heard a car pull into the driveway.

"It's Tonya and her mother," called Mom.

A few moments later, Tonya bounced into Seng's room without knocking. "Surprise!" she hollered, flinging herself across Seng's freshly made bed.

"Oh, hi," said Seng, trying not to sound annoyed. "What brings you here?"

With a wave of her hand, Tonya said, "My mom and I were on our way home from the grocery store, that's all."

Seng dusted while Tonya chattered. When

she started to dust her dresser, Tonya spotted the new ceramic lamb.

"Ooh, how pretty." Tonya jumped up off the bed and jerked the lamb off the dresser. "Where did you get such a cute little lamb?"

Seng cringed as Tonya inspected it. "Be careful," she warned.

But within seconds, Seng's worst fear came true. The ceramic figurine slipped from Tonya's grasp and shattered in dozens of tiny pieces at Seng's feet.

A look of horror crossed Tonya's face. Then without a word she ran out of the room and told her mother she needed to get home.

Seng didn't say good-bye to Tonya. Heartsick and angry, she swept up the mess.

"I don't know why Tonya wasn't more careful," Seng told her mother later. "And she never even apologized."

"I'm so sorry, honey," said Mom. "I know how much you treasured that lamb. Would you like me to pray with you?"

"Oh, Mom," sighed Seng. "I'm too sad to pray."

"I understand," Mom said. "Usually, that's when we need God's help the most."

**You, O Lord, have helped me
and comforted me.**

Psalm 86:17

▶▶▶▶▶▶▶▶▶▶▶▶▶▶

Something to Remember
God helps me through sad times.

Kwitcherbellyakin

Questions for Family Discussion

1. Do you think Seng had a right to be upset with Tonya?
2. Why did Seng's mom offer to pray with her?
3. How could God help Seng since the lamb was already broken?

Write a Family Prayer

_____

_____

_____

_____

SENG'S PRECIOUS LAMB

49

>>>>>>>>>>>>>>>>>>>>>>>>>>>>>>>>>>>>

AFTER THE STORM

One balmy September afternoon Jared and his brother, Trevor, decided to surprise their dad.

"You mow the grass, and I'll trim the hedges," said Jared. "We'll be done long before Dad gets home."

"Okay," agreed Trevor, "but we've got to hurry." He pointed to the gathering clouds. "Looks like we're going to get another storm."

One glance at the sky sent Jared scurrying for the garden shears. While Trevor mowed, Jared clipped the thick hedge that served as a fence around their spacious backyard.

After a while, silent raindrops dotted their shirts. "Hurry!" shouted Jared. "We're almost through."

Finishing not a minute too soon, the two brothers rushed into the shelter of their screened patio. There they watched the sky open up and bathe the trees, garden, and house with a refreshing rain.

Then, just minutes later, the sun streamed

154   **Kwitcherbellyakin**

through the branches again, its fingers of light reaching across the yard like a giant hand.

"That was a short rain," said Jared, scanning the sky for more clouds.

"Hey, look!" called Trevor, pointing to a patch of sky near an empty field. "God did it again!"

A brilliant rainbow splashed color across the horizon. "Pretty, huh?" said Jared.

"It's awesome," answered Trevor, "and the best part is what it means."

"Yeah," agreed Jared. "Remember God's promise to Noah when He gave the first rainbow? He promised He would never send another huge flood that would destroy the whole earth."

"Yeah, it's a good thing, too." Trevor laughed. "Otherwise, those hedge trimmers of Dad's that you left under that tree over there might be on their way to South America by now."

> **The LORD is faithful to all his promises and loving toward all he has made.**
>
> Psalm 145:13

▶▶▶▶▶▶▶▶▶▶▶▶

Something to Remember

God always keeps His promises.

Questions for Family Discussion:

1. Can you think of some promises God has given us?
2. Do you have a hard time keeping the promises you've made?
3. Would God change His mind and break one of His promises?
4. Have you promised to trust Jesus and obey Him? How are you doing?

Write a Family Prayer

_____

_____

_____

_____

50

▶▶▶▶▶▶▶▶▶▶▶▶▶▶▶▶▶▶▶▶▶▶▶▶▶▶▶▶▶▶▶▶

THE BEST PRESENT

As Tina got into the back of the station wagon with her friend Darlene, she twisted the strap of her purse nervously. She had never been to Sunday School before, but Darlene had been so nice to her that she couldn't turn down her invitation.

They arrived early, and Darlene excitedly introduced Tina to all her friends. "This is Tina," Darlene said proudly. "She's my neighbor from across the street in the yellow house."

Everyone made Tina feel at home. Their teacher, Mrs. Thomas, even gave her a glittery red pencil with *Welcome!* on it.

When Mrs. Thomas began her lesson, Tina listened carefully.

"The same God who hung the moon in the sky loves you personally," the teacher said, pointing to each boy and girl. "And the God who loves you personally sent His only Son to be your Savior." Mrs. Thomas explained that we've all done things that don't please God, but Jesus took our punishment, so that we can live with Him someday.

Hearing about God's love made Tina feel warm and good inside. She knew her parents loved her, but she had never heard that the God who created the whole world loved her.

After Sunday school, Darlene grabbed Tina's hand and led her down a corridor. "Come on," she said, "let's get a good seat up front for the church service."

Tina watched the choir walk in and sit in special seats facing the crowd. She listened to them sing about a Savior who loved them.

"Now here's the good part," Darlene whispered. "The pastor talks to just us kids at the beginning of his sermon."

Pastor Hardy came to the edge of the platform. "Boys and girls," he announced, smiling down at the children gathered eagerly in the front rows, "I have a special treat for one of you today." He held high a present wrapped in shiny paper.

"Ooh," the children all said together.

"Who would like to come up here and claim this present?" he asked.

Tina loved presents. Without thinking twice, she sprang to her feet and accepted the gift from Pastor Hardy. Returning to her seat, she unwrapped her gift. Inside was a picture of Jesus knocking at a beautiful garden gate. Tina turned to Darlene and smiled excitedly.

The pastor continued. "Because God loved us so much, He sent each of us a special present. He sent His very own Son to die on the cross for our sins." Pastor Hardy smiled tenderly at the boys and girls. "And when we hear Jesus knocking at the door of our hearts, and invite Him inside, we

are accepting the most precious gift ever given—
His gift of salvation."

Tina listened carefully to Pastor Hardy, and
that night as she lay in bed, she remembered what
he had said about God's present. *That gift must
have been hard for God to give*, she thought. *And
who wouldn't want a present like that? Next
Sunday I want to find out more.*

**Thanks be to God for his
indescribable gift!**
2 Corinthians 9:15

▶▶▶▶▶▶▶▶▶▶▶▶▶▶

Something to Remember

God sent Jesus as His special gift of love.

Questions for Family Discussion
1. Why does God call Jesus an indescribable gift?
2. Is God's special gift for everyone?
3. Whom could you invite to Sunday school?
4. What would you tell someone who wants to
   learn more about God's love?

Write a Family Prayer

_____

_____

_____

_____